What's Good?

Describing Your Public Library's Effectiveness

Thomas A. Childers *and* Nancy A. Van House

American Library Association

Chicago and London 1993

Cover designed by Charles Bozett

Composed by Charles Bozett in QuarkXPress

Printed on 50-pound Finch Opaque, a pH-neutral stock, and bound in 10-point C1S cover stock by IPC, St. Joseph, Michigan

The paper used in this publication meets the minimum requirements of American National Standard for Information Sciences—Permanence of Paper for Printed Library Materials, ANSI Z39.48-1984. ∞

Library of Congress Cataloging-in-Publication Data

Childers, Thomas, 1940–
      What's Good? : describing your public library's
effectiveness / by Thomas A. Childers and Nancy A.
Van House.
            p.   cm.
      Includes index.
      ISBN 0-8389-0617-6
      1. Public relations—Libraries—United States. 2. Public
libraries—United States—Administration. I. Van House,
Nancy A. II. Title.
Z716.3.C48   1993
021.7—dc20
                                                                  93-3683

Printed in the United States of America.

97 96 95 94 93   5 4 3 2 1

This book is dedicated to
John, Joey, and 148 oysters,
who all gave variously to the cause
at Point Reyes in the summer of '92.

Contents

5 The Public Library Effectiveness Study   28

Within, a brief description of the research on which is based a model of public library effectiveness.

6 A Model of Public Library Effectiveness (AMPLE)   33

In which is displayed and explicated a framework by which the manager may plan a program of representing the effectiveness of the library.

7 Applying AMPLE   54

On the use of AMPLE, with lessons from writers and practicing librarians about how to communicate with stakeholders, especially the critical external ones.

8 And, in Sum…   67

Wherein the major points made in the preceding are recapped and the implications for the library future are drawn.

Appendices

Bibliography   89

Index   91

This Book Is about . . .

Our mission is to (1) define effectiveness for the public library and (2) provide guidelines for assessing the library's effectiveness and communicating same to the library's stakeholders.

> The impatient reader can go directly to chapter 8, "And, in Sum . . . ," for a capsule view of the book and its parts, then move directly to the parts of greatest interest.

Organizations in the public sector are in danger. Public libraries are in danger.

The dangers are many, and they threaten every public organization with the possibility of reduced usership, reduced funding, and reduced political and social support. The story of the assorted dangers has been told often. Their impact has been felt by every organization, from sanitation departments to arts leagues to . . . libraries.

The dangers we speak of are largely external. The environment that sustains the public library organization—and every other public organization—is the same environment that threatens it. Yet the threats themselves, the dangers to organizational existence, imply what a public organization—a library—might do to maintain its health in that nurturing yet perilous environment.

> *. . . organizations survive to the extent they are effective.* (Pfeffer and Salancik 1978, 2)

Management must make sure that the organization *is effective.*

Just as important, the organization must *be seen* as effective. That is, the organization must successfully *represent*—demonstrate, declare—its effectiveness to the environment. *Being* effective and *representing* effectiveness are two different things; but they are equally important.

What's Good? is about the two component parts of representing the organization's effectiveness: *assessing,* or gathering, appropriate intelligence about the state of the library organization; and *communicating,* or transmitting, that intelligence in a useful and influential way to the library's stakeholders. That is the theme of the book. Moreover, it concentrates on representing the library to the *external* stakeholders—those outside the library who directly or indirectly affect the library's present and future.

Making the organization more effective is important, but that is not the aim of this book, except insofar as the very acts of assessing effectiveness better and communicating that assessment better can make the organization more effective. That is, in a circular way, better assessment and better communication of effectiveness are themselves components of effectiveness.

The mission of this book is to offer a framework that will help the library manager develop a program of assessment and strategies for communicating that assessment to the library's environment—in short, a scheme for representing the public library organization.

Howard Rubin recently published a recipe for the organization that wants to develop an evaluation program:

- Identify all audiences for measurement.
- Analyze the measurement needs of each audience.
- Produce a map that cross-references audiences to needs.
- Produce a map that cross-references needs to possible metrics.
- Decide which candidate metrics to use.
- Establish priorities and a phased implementation plan.

(Rubin 1991, 79)

The "maps" that Rubin recommends are exactly what we offer here: a framework for deciding how to assess and communicate the organization's—in this case, the public library's—effectiveness. The framework is called "A Model of Public Library Effectiveness" (AMPLE). In contrast to the popular *Output Measures for Public Libraries* (Van House and others 1987), which concentrates on service outputs, AMPLE offers a broad array of assessment points, from inputs through outputs, and moves toward service outcomes, or impact. In doing so, AMPLE recognizes that a *range* of assessment points is required in order to represent a public library's effectiveness fully to its various stakeholder groups.

Chapter 1 is about organizational effectiveness: what it is and why we care. It begins by asking, "How do you tell a good library from a bad library?" and discusses the beginnings of an answer by looking at past approaches to effectiveness in the management literature.

Chapter 2 is about how to gauge effectiveness, and it links effectiveness to such slippery ideas as evaluation, measurement, qualitative and quantitative evidence, and the systems approach to organizations.

Chapter 3 presents the steps that the public library field has taken to improve the ways of assessing and communicating goodness, including strategic planning, measurement, personnel appraisal, and budgeting.

Chapter 4 considers what makes the public library what it is and how its particular characteristics might affect the way library managers depict its effectiveness.

Chapter 5 briefly presents the methods and key findings of *The Public Library Effectiveness Study*, which forms the research basis of this book.

Chapter 6 unveils "A Model of Public Library Effectiveness" (AMPLE): a framework by which the manager may plan a program of assessing public library effectiveness.

Chapter 7 is about using AMPLE to communicate. The library has a number of key stakeholder groups who must be identified and whose particular needs and preferences determine how to talk to them about effectiveness.

Finally, Chapter 8 recaps the major arguments of the book and discusses their implications for public library management.

This book is for library managers. It addresses directly the executive level of the library organization and emphasizes the organization's inter-action with the external environment. However, much of the discussion and many of the recommendations in the book can be applied to internal decisions regarding the operation of the library. And most of the content can be applied to subunits (departments) of the library, such as technical processing or reference, if one extrapolates, viewing the subunit as the "organization" and the overall organization as the "external environment." Branches of library systems can benefit particularly well from this discussion. Their external environment encompasses both the larger library system and the external world.

The book's venue is the public library, for that is the context in which our major research and developmental work have taken place. Nonetheless, many of the principles and conclusions drawn in this volume will translate to other types of libraries: academic, special, and school. These libraries, too, share common problems of assessing their effectiveness and communicating it internally and externally; only the particulars differ. Moreover, the principles underlying the book are applicable to other public sector organizations.

What's Good? is based on our 40 collective years of experience in evaluating and studying libraries; consulting with library staffs and directors; and, particularly, our recent research on public library effectiveness. That research can be found in the companion book to this, *The Public Library Effectiveness Study* (Van House and Childers 1993), a nationwide study to develop a definition of public library effectiveness.

Acknowledgments

The book was nurtured by many things:

- The sites of Philadelphia, Berkeley, San Francisco, San Antonio, Inverness (California), Toronto, Sheffield, London, Brighton, and several airplanes, which inspired the writing;
- The librarians, community leaders, local officials, library friends, trustees, library users, and other subjects of the study;
- The people who advised us during the study: Kathy Arnold, Pottstown (Pennsylvania) Public Library; Herbert Davis, past trustee, Baltimore County Public Library; Sandy Dolnick, Friends of Libraries USA; Fred Philipp, Ingram Library Services; Eleanor Jo Rodger, Urban Libraries Council; Eliott Shelkrot, Free Library of Philadelphia; and Kathryn

Stephanoff, Allentown (Pennsylvania) Public Library;

- At Drexel, Dr. Howard White, for his statistical advice, and Rebecca Fisher and Kathleen H. Turner, who assisted in or oversaw many facets of the study with extraordinary skill; and Sue Easun, who competently and gracefully held up the Berkeley end;
- At Berkeley, Vickie Parker, proofreader extraordinaire;
- At the University of Minnesota, Dr. George D'Elia, for additional advice on analysis;
- The kindness of non-strangers who reviewed and commented on the draft: Karen Krueger, Janesville (Wisconsin) Public Library; Amy Owen, Utah State Library; and Dr. Jane Robbins, University of Wisconsin;
- The U.S. Department of Education, Office of Educational Research & Improvement, which underwrote most of the study from which this book developed.

References

Pfeffer, Jeffrey, and Gerald R. Salancik. 1978. *The External Control of Organizations.* New York: Harper and Row.

Rubin, Howard. 1991. "Inch into Measurement." *Computerworld* (April 15): 79.

Van House, Nancy A., and Thomas Childers. 1993. *The Public Library Effectiveness Study: The Complete Report.* Chicago: American Library Association.

Van House, Nancy A., Mary Jo Lynch, Charles R. McClure, Douglas L. Zweizig, and Eleanor Jo Rodger. 1987. *Output Measures for Public Libraries,* 2nd ed. Chicago: American Library Association.

What *Is* Good?

In which is asked the question, "How do you tell a good library from a bad library?" and in which is laid down the beginning of the answer.

> The real essence of appearing competent is for managers to demonstrate that their agency is special—that they do good things that other agencies do not do and that they set standards that other agencies would do well to follow.
> (Chase and Reveal 1983, 51)

The Quintessential Question

"How can you tell a good X from a bad X?" The question has probably been on the mind of humankind since the realization that there was more than one X. We are fundamentally evaluative animals and, just as we evaluate all things, we evaluate organizations. They are supposed to accomplish something, to be in some way good for something, and someone has always been there to ask the question, "How good?"

> Organizations are supposed to be good; libraries are supposed to be good.

The goodness question is implied in attempts to describe the benefits derived from organizations, to explain their impact, to set their budgets, to restructure them, to change their operations, to count their accomplishments, and on rare occasion to disband them. The Gross Domestic Product is a way of representing the goodness of the national economy. Number of welfare cases handled and number of indigent people fed are ways of representing goodness for certain human service organizations. Net profits is a way to represent goodness for profit-making organizations. Win-loss records represent goodness for sports teams.

Organizations are supposed to be good; libraries are supposed to be good. The question of goodness translates in today's management literature into the subject of *effectiveness*.

Pfeffer and Salancik define effectiveness this way:

> The effectiveness of an organization is its ability to create acceptable outcomes and actions. . . . it reflects both an assessment of the usefulness of what is being done and of the resources that are being consumed by the organization (Pfeffer and Salancik 1978, 11).

This book treats effectiveness very broadly, even more broadly than they. In this chapter, you will encounter effectiveness from a number of points of view—all of them valid. To put all points of view into a single definition, it has to be simple and broad: *goodness, or achieving success, the quality of performance,* conceived in many different ways. The important point, to be dealt with shortly, is that the idea of goodness is multiform. It is inclusive rather than exclusive.

> Effectiveness is:
> • goodness,
> • achieving success, and
> • the quality of performance.

We can distinguish between effectiveness and efficiency, defining effectiveness as impact on the consumer or user and efficiency as the economy with which "effect" is achieved. Commonly, outputs and outcomes are emphasized in effectiveness. However, the broader definition of effectiveness embraces all aspects of the organization. One can view effectiveness in terms of organizational inputs (resources), processes (activities), outputs (products and services), outcomes (impact on clients and community), and interactions with the social, political, and economic environment. For organizations, effectiveness can be assessed at the level of the individual, the work unit, the department, or the whole organization. Our concern in this book is the latter: *organization-level effectiveness.*

Why Should Effectiveness Concern Us?

> *The government manager has one final responsibility: to maintain the health of the organization by seeing that it adjusts to new political demands.*
> (Heymann 1987, 11)

There are several reasons why the public has become increasingly interested in effectiveness in the public sector:

- Public services are increasing in number and complexity as society becomes more complex.
- The cost of providing public goods and services is rising; tax revenues are not growing at the same pace as demand for public services, especially critical public services like health and public safety; and there is more competition for the tax dollar.
- The public sector is increasingly required to fund services mandated by the public, leaving little money for discretionary services.
- Society is concerned with return on its investment in services; similarly, society, through the political process, is increasingly inclined to fund critical public services and to ignore others.
- The destinies of public organizations seem to be tied more closely to a changing political scene, because decisions cannot be made from a solely analytical base.

These many forces, bearing heavily on the organization's future, are the reasons for interest in goodness, and they are largely external. In sum, they amount to scarcity of resource and, consequently, increased competition. Society's interest in effectiveness is especially pronounced in the public sector, where tax revenues fund products and services whose value is not tested by the market; and where one group (taxpayers) often pays for services used by another (beneficiaries). Fears of public sector waste are a recurrent theme in the American public's

relationships to its government. Public decision-makers, such as city councils, county managers, budget authorities, voters, and corporate donors, continually seek assurances that public money is spent in a worthwhile way.

Society's interest in effectiveness naturally triggers the manager's interest in effectiveness. Society hires the manager to run a good organization. Part of the manager's job description is telling society how good the organization is. Also whetting the manager's interest in effectiveness is the fact that the use of strategic marketing has become a popular means for increasing organizational performance. The manager needs to know how the organization is faring vis-á-vis the market and the competition, and this calls for self-assessment and comparison with others in the environment.

> Effectiveness is a concern because resources are scarce.

Although there are various meanings of "worthwhile spending," the governors (external overseers, such as elected and appointed officials and trustees) and funders of libraries—and in some cases the taxpayers who support the services—increasingly want more information about the impact of public programs and the dollars that support them. They want to know that:

- the dollars have been spent responsibly;
- the programs are of value; and
- they are funding an optimum, or at least good, mix of functions.

The twin matters of economy of operation and "value" both address the accountability of the organization to society.

These many reasons for the concern about effectiveness have become more compelling in recent years. Responding to the pressures, public library leadership has acted to improve the assessment of library goodness, leading to a twenty-year effort to develop better means of setting direction for public libraries and assessing achievement. More of this in chapter 3.

Advances in information technology and services are going to mean that libraries have increasing opportunities to provide useful, interesting, and attractive, but costly, services. Quite apart from other social and economic pressures, these developments will exacerbate the library's scarcity problems. More and more may be done, with (probably) fixed or declining resources.

Internal and external decision-makers will have to choose how best to use the library's limited funds.

Approaches to Effectiveness

The management literature offers four main approaches to looking at effectiveness. Taken together, they conjure a broad perspective and lead to a comprehensive idea of organizational effectiveness. The four approaches, or models, proclaim the multidimensionality of effectiveness and the validity of multiple viewpoints. The different approaches emphasize different things about the organization, posing, as it were, questions that might be asked when assessing an organization:

- To what extent does the organization achieve its *goals* (input, process, output, or outcome goals)?
- To what extent is the organization a *healthy operating unit?*
- To what extent can the organization capture from the external environment the *resources* needed to survive or thrive?
- To what extent are the various *stakeholders'* priorities met?

To the seasoned library manager, these questions may seem obvious; but it is likely that most managers emphasize one or another of them.

The questions are reflected in the descriptions of the four major *models of effectiveness* found in the management literature. The models provide some of the basis for developing a comprehensive framework of library effectiveness later in this book.

> *Goal.* The *goal* model views effectiveness in terms of the organization's achievement of specific ends (Cameron 1981). It stresses outputs and productivity, such as consumption of services and units of work per staff member. "To what extent does the organization achieve its goals?"

> *Process.* The *process* model says that organizations do not exist solely to attain their goals (Cameron 1981). They are also social groups seeking to survive and maintain their equilibrium. Thus, effectiveness is measured by internal processes and organizational health (for instance, internal communication and degree of staff turnover) as well as by goal attainment. "To what extent is the organization a healthy operating unit?"

> *Systems resource.* The *systems resource* model emphasizes the organization's need to secure resources from its environment (Scott 1987). Relationships with external resources and their controllers—such as those with power in the budgetary process or the ability to pass a tax referendum—thus become the basis for judging effectiveness. "To what extent can the organization capture from the external environment (say, the funding body) the resources needed to survive or thrive?"

> *Multiple constituencies.* The *multiple constituencies* model is concerned with the organization's constituent groups (Zammuto 1984). It defines effectiveness as the degree to which the needs and expectations of strategic constituencies, such as certain user groups or leaders in the community, are met. It differs from the systems resource model in that the constituencies to be satisfied are not necessarily the power elite. "To what extent are the various stakeholders happy with the organization?"

The models emphasize different aspects of the organization's effectiveness. They should be seen as overlapping rather than contradictory. Different approaches may be appropriate under different organizational circumstances. Different constituent groups of the same organization, and even different members of a constituent group, may adopt different approaches to evaluating an organization's effectiveness. For instance, a small stockholder may view Widgetcorp's effectiveness in terms of payment of short-term dividends, while a large stockholder may see it in terms of long-term market share. Moreover, a *comprehensive* framework of organizational assessment requires—if we accept the experience reflected in the management literature—all four approaches.

An underlying theme of these approaches is that there is no single definition of effectiveness for an organization and no single person or group that defines it. There are multiple groups to be satisfied (the multiple constituencies approach), external interests that control the critical external resources needed (the systems resource approach), activities inside the organization that are vital in delivering products and services (the process approach), and various goals pursued by the same organization (the goals approach).

> Effectiveness is largely a *point of view.*

In addition to agreeing that effectiveness is a multidimensional concept, the management literature also has come to advocate that no single definition of or approach to organizational effectiveness is inherently *most valid*. The various viewpoints of an organization's effectiveness are *all* valid. Thus, representing the organization's effectiveness fully can be a complex matter. And thus, the manager must offer different representations of the organization's effectiveness in order to address that complexity—those various points of view and the many facets of the library organization.

If effectiveness is essentially a point of view, it is conceivable that there are as many views of a single organization's effectiveness as there are people. But that doesn't help the library manager. There isn't time or money enough to identify everyone's point of view. And the points of view would be so many that they would cloud rather than clarify. The question for the library manager, then, is: Whose assessment matters? Whose goals and criteria, whose opinions, whose vision, does the manager listen and respond to?

> A major aspect of library effectiveness is *representing* the library to key stakeholders.

One useful answer is: the stakeholders who can influence the organization's survival—the *key stakeholders*. (Pfeffer and Salancik 1978). The organization has an internal life, of course, filled with the activities of the working day that produce the services and products that the customer consumes. But it also has an external life that is at least equally important, a context that is political, economic, and social. Thus, an organization's stakeholders will be found internally and externally.

For the library manager, effectiveness is not only a matter of running an effective organization. It is equally a matter of *representing* the library's effectiveness to key stakeholders—that is, *assessing* the library and *communicating* that assessment. Representing it well means the manager has to identify the key stakeholders in the library's future, determine their priorities, and decide how to speak to them.

Conclusion

This chapter has identified effectiveness—its measurement and its representation—as a critical issue for library managers. A number of definitions or models of effectiveness exist in the literature. We suggest that the most useful approach is not to pick among them, but to use them all: to see the validity in each and to see that, taken together, they suggest a broad definition of effectiveness. Many people are involved in assessing a library's effectiveness, which means that offering many points of view is in the best interests of the library manager.

The next chapter continues to look at the concept of effectiveness and how it relates to evaluation. Chapter 4 considers further the nature of public sector organizations—and public libraries—and what that implies for statements about their effectiveness.

References

Cameron, Kim. 1981. "Domains of Organizational Effectiveness in Colleges and Universities." *Academy of Management Journal* 24: 25–47.

Chase, Gordon, and Elizabeth C. Reveal. 1983. *How to Manage in the Public Sector.* Reading, Mass.: Addison-Wesley.

Heymann, Philip B. 1987. *Politics of Public Management.* New Haven, Conn.: Yale University Press.

Pfeffer, Jeffrey, and Gerald R. Salancik. 1978. *The External Control of Organizations.* New York: Harper & Row.

Scott, W. Richard. 1987. *Organizations: Rational, Natural, and Open Systems.* Englewood Cliffs, N.J.: Prentice-Hall.

Zammuto, Raymond F. 1984. "A Comparison of Multiple Constituency Models of Organizational Effectiveness." *Academy of Management Review* 9: 606–16.

Effectiveness and Evaluation

In which effectiveness is linked to such slippery ideas as evaluation, measurement, qualitative and quantitative evidence, and the "systems" way of looking at things.

Measuring vs. Evaluating

Evaluation is the assessment of goodness. It consists of comparing the organization's current performance against some standard or set of expectations. Evaluation has two parts: the collection of information, or evidence, about the organization's performance; and the comparison of this information to some set of criteria. The collection of information is not in itself evaluation: a critical component of evaluation is the exercise of judgment in which criteria are applied to the organization's current reality.

Evaluation = Judgment

The outcome of the evaluation—the conclusions reached about effectiveness—depends on both the criteria and the evidence used. The choice of criteria is based on the decision-maker's definition of effectiveness: the different approaches described in chapter 1 often produce differing criteria. In the same way, different points of view may produce different criteria. Some observers of the public library, for example, may place a priority on services to children and be particularly interested in criteria that reflect this. Others may be more interested in services to other groups from the community.

Evaluation can rest on a wide range of information. The goal, of course, is a reasonably accurate picture of the organization, and a variety of evidence can be used to create this picture. The evidence can be quantitative or qualitative and systematically or idiosyncratically derived.

Quantitative evidence is measurement data. It can be expressed in numbers, such as number of circulations, users, or materials. *Qualitative* evidence is more subjective and impressionistic and is unquantified. But it is no less valid—for example, a visual assessment of the cleanliness of physical facilities or the overall helpfulness of the staff.

Surveys sometimes turn qualitative assessments quantitative. Instead of recording the helpfulness impressions of one user or a few selected users, you could survey the users systematically, recording their helpfulness ratings on a scale from 1 (most helpful) to 5 (least helpful). A mean friendliness rating of 1.3 does not have an objective meaning like a mean circulation per user of 1.3 would have. That is, it has a qualitative base—an opinion or impression offered many times and counted (quantified).

Systematically collected evidence is intended to reflect a general reality—all instances of a phenomenon (a census), such as a count of all circulation transactions, or a representative portion of a phenomenon (a sample), such as a random sample of circulation transactions. Opinion evidence that is systematically collected, as in a survey of public opinion, can fulfill either the census or the sample functions as well as objective numeric data can.

Idiosyncratic evidence is collected so as to reflect particular points of view, like the opinion of the president of the board or the experiences of a few new library users, not to reflect a general reality.

Whether quantitative or qualitative, systematic or idiosyncratic, evidence is subjected to one or more criteria. A criterion may be hard—a number, as embodied in an objective like "We want to achieve a circulation of 4.5 items per capita per year." Or it may be soft—an ambiguous value, such as "The online catalog should be easy for the user to find things in." (How easy is "easy"?)

> Evaluation = weighing evidence against criteria.

Evaluation is the process of holding evidence against criteria (figure 1). "How does the actual circulation per capita per year compare with our objective? Did we do well, or not?" "Were we able to make the online catalog easier to use?"

The important point is that evidence, however hard or objective, does not make the judgment for you. Hard evidence may contribute to an evaluation of goodness, but it does not, in itself, perform the evaluation (make the judgment). Both in formulating a quantified objective ("generate 65,000 reference queries a year") and in determining the library's success on that objective, the act of *judging* has occurred. Setting the objective, or choosing the criteria, requires deciding *what* "good" is. Comparing evidence to the criteria is judging how good the library is in one of its aspects or another. The purpose of evaluation is always the assessment of *how* good.

This is true in evaluating the *effectiveness* of an organization. The subjective act of judging is the essence of evaluating effectiveness. How good is the library?

If, as we said in chapter 1, there is no single definer or judge of effectiveness for an organization, then evaluation requires communication with a multitude of constituent groups or stakeholders who have differing concerns, or criteria, and will make different judgments. Thus, in order to communicate with the key stakeholders, one wants a *broad* and *flexible* idea of which evaluative information is useful in describing the library (the subject of chapter 6, "A Model of Public Library Effectiveness," and AMPLE itself) and how to communicate to the particular stakeholder group (taken up in chapter 4, "The Nature of the Library Organization and Implications for Effectiveness").

Dimensions, Indicators, and Measures of Goodness

Several key words are pivotal in discussing organizational effectiveness. Unfortunately, virtually all are used with assorted meanings in the literature and in conversation. In order to move through the rest of this book with reasonable ease, it is necessary to stabilize them. The definitions that follow refer to figure 2, "Dimensions, Indicators, and Measures," and figure 3, "Dimensions, Indicators, and Measures Illustrated."

Effectiveness is goodness. It is equivalent to the quality of performance. In this book, effectiveness is applied to the organization as a whole; but, as mentioned in chapter 1, everything that will be presented can be adjusted for use at the subunit level, such as children's services or technical processing.

A *dimension* of effectiveness is a broad aspect of performance that is monitored in assessing effectiveness. To take an example from another field, three appropriate dimensions of effectiveness for a police department might be "crime prevention," "community relations," and "departmental efficiency" (Jobson and Schneck 1982). In public libraries, dimensions of effectiveness might include "information delivery," "community relations," "access to services," or "administrative processes."

A dimension, in turn, is made up of more specific items of effectiveness, called *indicators*. An indicator of the dimension "crime prevention" might be "crime rate." An indicator of the library dimension "access to services" might be"adequacy of parking"; an indicator of the dimension "administrative processes" might be "written policies."

The indicator becomes concrete when translated into a *measure* of effectiveness. The indicator

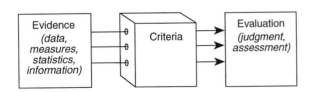

Figure 1. Evidence, Criteria, Evaluation

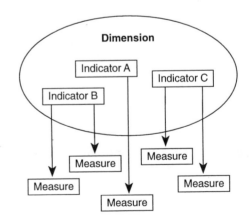

Figure 2. Dimensions, Indicators, and Measures

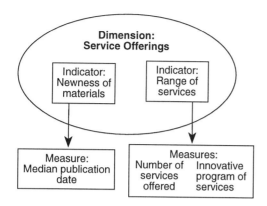

Figure 3. Dimensions, Indicators, and Measures Illustrated

suggests a concept on which to focus a review of effectiveness; the measure offers a specific means (measure, scale, data element) by which to gain that focus. To be used as evidence of effectiveness, an indicator must be turned into a means by which the organization may be described. Thus, a measure of the indicator "adequacy of parking" might be the number of parking spaces or user satisfaction with parking accommodations; and a measure of the indicator "extent to which policies are written" might be the number of pages of written service policy or a list of topics on which the library has formally adopted policies.

A major fallibility of a measure, no matter how quantitative or "objective," is that it is not the thing itself, but a metaphor. "Shades" is a metaphor for sunglasses. "Rock" is a metaphor for the hard lumpy grey thing over there. An IQ score is a metaphor for intelligence. A *measure* of effectiveness is a metaphor for the actual effectiveness of an organization. At best, it approxi-

> It is better to be roughly right than exactly wrong.
> (Koenig 1980, 39)

mates the thing it represents. It stands for the thing, but is not the thing, as circulation count stands for actual circulation, or as number of parking spaces stands for adequacy of parking.

The measure is rarely perfect. That is, there is rarely a one-to-one match between the measure and what one wants to measure. There is almost always a discrepancy between the measure and reality, or between the measure and the thing one wants to measure. A measure like circulation count is very close in concept to the real thing, actual circulation. However, flaws in counting regularly lead to inaccuracies in the

count; and the measure thus becomes discrepant with actual circulation. In contrast, number of parking spaces explains only part of the concept of "adequacy of parking." Thus, the measure and the thing itself are discrepant, regardless of the accuracy of count. It is humbling, but realistic, to assume that measures are flawed and to accept that as a challenge for improvement.

Ultimately, we would like to know what causes effectiveness; what actions bring about effectiveness? These are *determinants*—the things that make an organization better than it was before, or better than another organization. Managers investigate determinants and make assumptions about them all the time. Researchers do too. They try to discover the things that influence the indicators and measures of effectiveness. For example, does the training of a librarian influence the quality of reference service? Does the amount of money spent on new materials influence the number of people using the library? Does the form of city government affect the tax base of the library? Some determinants are things that managers can manipulate to bring about—or try to bring about—improvement, such as circulation loan period. Some are not manipulable, such as the ethnic mix of a neighborhood.

While determinants is critical in the chain of effectiveness concepts, there is little research that has established the determinants of effectiveness in libraries. Therefore, we concentrate in this book on indicators and measures and leave determinants to the wisdom of the local practitioner or manager and to future research.

Evaluating through Numbers and through Stories

For the past 15 years, the public library field has concentrated on developing objective measures that embrace service consumption and service quality. The aim was to *quantify* library "products" in a meaningful way, to describe libraries in quantitative terms related to what they *accomplished*, rather than what resources (including human) were used up. The focus was on measures, numbers, counts, tallies—on how many items (books, journals, programs, etc.) were *available* and how many items were *consumed* (borrowed, attended, located, etc.) by the users. This focus produced an important advance, in that it offered a fairly comprehensive package of quantified outputs to the field.

> The whole picture of library goodness requires both a paint-by-numbers approach and impressionism.

However, an additional insight emerged in the course of *The Public Library Effectiveness Study.* In our talks with library directors, local officials, and some community leaders, it became clear that, while numbers are necessary and useful, something else may be as compelling in representing the library to external stakeholders: anecdotes, or stories of organizational achievement. These are essentially stories of impact that the library has achieved in the past year: teaching the skill of reading aloud to an indigent young mother; providing the information on trash removal innovations that influenced city council legislation. Indeed, the story can be negative as well as positive, such as the impact of inadequate book funds on one student's homework.

We learned that representing the library's goodness is not limited to numbers. Stories may have as much impact on decision-makers as data. Perhaps more. This idea will be developed in chapter 7, where using data and stories in talking to stakeholders is discussed.

Evaluating via the General Systems Model

In considering organizations and their goodness, a useful framework is the general systems model. In fact, this framework has been used in guiding most evaluation efforts. The open systems model of effectiveness, which was discussed in chapter 1, springs from the general systems model. We take a slight pause here in order to put the process of evaluation in context, using the general systems model.

The general systems model has been used for decades to describe the components of systems of all types and levels, ranging from the system called the Milky Way to the system called a library to the system called your left big toe.

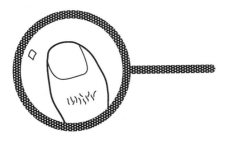

At its simplest level, a system is a nexus of interacting elements. The major pieces of a system are:

- inputs, the resources that are needed to support the system (such as the nutrients needed for a human cell, or library revenues);
- processes, the activities that transform the inputs to outputs (such as metabolism, or the library's book preparation activities);
- outputs, the product of the system (such as heat from the metabolic process, or library circulation);
- outcomes, the impact of the system's outputs on the external environment (such as growth of the toe, or the library's impact on individual or community);
- feedback, the means whereby information related to output or outcome is "fed back" into the input or the process stage of the system, for purposes of correction (such as lack of oxygen, or the community's response to a library program); and
- environment, the context within which the system exists—an environment that provides economic and material resources, markets, political forces, technologies, competitors, and the like (such as a whole foot and its surrounding shoe, or the political, economic, and social elements that surround the library).

The model is arranged as shown in figure 4.

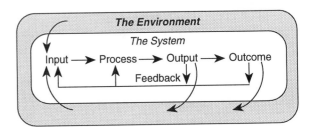

Figure 4. The General Systems Model

The systems model is a major tool for analyzing virtually any system in virtually any discipline—from medical research to thermodynamics to futurology to information delivery mechanisms—since it lets you see the system in terms of interactions among its main component parts: raw materials (input), transformations of these raw materials (process), resulting products and their consumption (output) and their effects (outcome), and information about these things that sustains and improves the system (feedback).

In viewing an organization, one would like to see all parts of the system. However, outputs and outcomes pose exceptional problems. They are the least easily observed of all the elements of the system. They are often a product of not just the system under study, but other, sometimes unknown, factors which may be far removed from the system in time and place. For instance, a branch library's rate of circulation may relate more to the educational level of the community than to the policies or practices of the library. In the case of many public sector organizations, such as libraries, the desired outcomes, such as the nature of impact on the individual or community, are often not even articulated. Thus, there are no criteria against which to hold evidence, and no suggestion of which evidence to collect.

Using a library to illustrate the elements of the general systems model, one can broadly identify:

- inputs: money, staff, materials, and physical plant;
- processes: staff, machine, and building activities;
- outputs: services, materials, and facilities consumed; and
- outcomes: use of information; change in the client or community.

See figure 5.

Feedback can occur in the form of measures of output or outcome that are used, for instance, to make changes in budget or staffing requests (input) or in the continuing education of staff or handling of reference inquiries (process). Feedback also comes in non-quantitative forms, such as letters from users, patrons' conversations with library staff, live reactions to library presentations at community meetings, and so on.

The systems model offers a simple framework for analyzing an organization's effectiveness in a comprehensive way. It can serve almost as a checklist of the various broad areas to consider in evaluating and communicating effectiveness. To the extent that an organization—a library— is assessing and communicating its effective-

ness in all of the four system areas, the organization is more likely to be representing its effectiveness fully.

Employing the systems approach, Orr (1973) presents a useful conception of how the various aspects of organizational performance relate to each other in libraries. In figure 6, adapted from Orr, the "quality" of resources (i.e., quantity of dollars) and organizational effort (capability) are related—albeit loosely—to the value of services delivered.

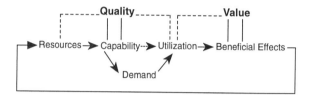

Figure 6. The Orr Model of Input and Output

However, the links among resources, quality, and value are neither direct nor obvious. Libraries have always been required to demonstrate that they are operating at the lowest possible cost, or at a reasonable cost, or at least honestly. Historically, the watchful eyes of the funders and controllers of the public library (city hall, trustees, taxpayers, etc.) have been trained on the spending of the resources because this is the most measurable element of Orr's model. There has been much less focus on quality or value of what the library delivers, at least in part because this is so much harder to measure. In our years of interviewing library managers we have seen more than one public library board that interprets its job as protecting the taxpayer from tax increases, rather than achieving good (quality, or valuable) library services. And we have seen modestly funded libraries achieve high performance.

In part, the lack of accounting for quality and value results from the difficulty of knowing what quality and value are. The term "value," alone, could be interpreted in several ways:

- positive impact on the individual user,
- positive political visibility,
- positive social impact, and
- positive economic impact.

The systems model is useful for a first look at effectiveness. But it is coarsegrained. As we will find out later, a finer grained framework will be needed to set the library on the road to full representation of its goodness.

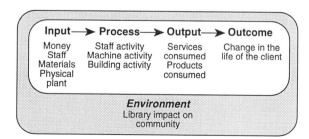

Figure 5. The Systems View of the Library

Conclusion

Evaluation, then, is the exercise of judgment in which evidence of organizational performance is compared to criteria. The evidence used may be of many types, as may be the criteria. A dimension of effectiveness is a broad aspect of an organization's performance that is monitored in doing evaluation. A dimension is made up of one or more indicators. An indicator becomes concrete when operationalized by a measure. Measures are rarely perfect representations of their indicators and dimensions. And we should not limit ourselves to quantitative data; qualitative information and anecdotes can be useful and persuasive.

The general systems model gives us a way to evaluate the relationship among the components of the organization and between the organization and its environment.

References

Jobson, J. D., and Rodney Schneck. 1982. "Constituent Views of Organizational Effectiveness: Evidence from Police Organizations." *Academy of Management Journal* 25: 25–46.

Koenig, Michael E. D. 1980. *Budgeting Techniques for Libraries and Information Centers.* New York: Special Libraries Association, 39.

Orr, Richard H. 1973. "Measuring the Goodness of Library Services: A General Framework for Considering Quantitative Measures." *Journal of Documentation* 29, no. 3: 315–32.

Advances on the Goodness Question in Libraries

3

Wherein is shown how the public library field has taken steps to improve the way libraries assess and communicate goodness. The steps include strategic planning, measurement, personnel appraisal, and budgeting systems.

Thinkers about general management have advanced the degree to which organizational effectiveness can be represented. They have created tools that directly or indirectly speak to goodness—tools that help management to:

- set direction, for the long or short term, and
- control movement in that direction.

The tools relate to money, the future, and people: budgeting, planning, managing personnel, and—most directly to the point of assessing effectiveness—measuring. While their ultimate purpose is to make the organization more effective, they are also used to *represent* the organization's effectiveness.

Public library management, too, has developed a repertoire of tools that help set direction and control organizational activities. The major advances have come in planning and measurement. Important, though lesser, advances have occurred in a number of other areas; for this book, budgeting and performance appraisal are singled out to illustrate tools that were designed for directing and controlling, but are also useful in assessing and communicating effectiveness.

In both general management and public library management, the tools that have been developed are only partial answers to the goodness question, for they each tend to represent the organization in a particular way (spending, goals, personnel, and so on). To this extent, they offer limited views of goodness. Taken together, they begin to create a patchwork picture of the organization. The purpose of this book is to offer a more comprehensive view.

Planning and Measurement

Before the 1970s, the explicit criteria by which the effectiveness of many public libraries was judged consisted of national standards: a public library should have so many volumes per capita, have so many dollars per capita, offer so many service hours per week, and so on. The last set of national standards for U.S. public libraries was issued by the Public Library Association (1967). Portentously, the introduction to the 1967 edition indicated that such standards needed rethinking and a new approach.

Thus was launched a concerted movement to "localize" the standards by which public libraries are evaluated, to establish *locally* the criteria by which libraries are judged. This has translated into two main thrusts:

planning and
measuring achievement in terms of the plan.

More specifically, the movement for local determination of library goodness, beginning in the early 1970s and continuing into the present day, embraces:

- assessing the local community needs (pre-planning);
- developing a concrete set of objectives and strategies for meeting those needs (planning); and
- measuring the achievement of those objectives.

The localization movement became the major agenda item of the Public Library Association in the mid-1970s and continues in its prominence today. The movement sought simple and flexible aids to planning and measurement. It appears to have succeeded. As this work evolved, a broad professional consensus developed. The result has been widespread acceptance by the public library community of the need to plan and measure (and, subsequently, evaluate) for the local situation.

In the next few pages, we will treat planning and measurement in reverse order, to show the historic line of the two developments.

Measurement

For decades, a premise that underlay much management thought and research was that somewhere out there was a relatively simple measure—probably uniform, universal, and unifaceted—that would describe the effectiveness of organizations, generally; and that enough research and thought should reveal what it was; and more research and thought would reveal how to attain it. If there weren't a simple effectiveness measure for *all* organizations, there was probably a simple one for all organizations of a given type—libraries, for example, or at least all public libraries. Thousands of publications across a range of fields over the last several decades bear witness to the search for what might be called the "Grail of Goodness."

The library profession joined the crusade. The quest for the Grail of *Library* Goodness (Buckland 1988] has resulted in thousands of publications and unpublished in-house reports that sought better ways of describing library effectiveness. These writings have often obscured the essential point: What is the essence of the library? To choose a measure of success requires first a *definition* of success—i.e., of effectiveness.

The writings have included:

- use and user studies;
- cost-benefit and cost-effectiveness analyses;
- reports of library statistics;
- evaluations of library collections;
- works on measurable objectives and output measures;
- statements on library standards;
- writings on planning for libraries;
- debates about the essential public library purpose; and
- proposals for alternative budget systems.

All of this literature has aimed to describe the goodness of the library in one way or another.

Obviously, there has been a wide variety of approaches to and measures of effectiveness.

In recent years, however, it has slowly dawned on the writers and readers of the management literature that the Grail of Goodness may be like the original Grail—a compelling, shimmering illusion. The idea of effectiveness has matured. It is now seen as situational, organic, multifaceted, and a point of view.

The library field has echoed the management field in proliferating articles and reports on effectiveness. The mass of library publications suggests that library goodness is not likely to be reflected in a single all-purpose measure; that it has many facets, or dimensions; that it is not likely to be defined in the same way for all libraries, or even for all libraries of a given type; and that it may be defined differently for each different interest group.

Measures and the Systems Model

For most of the history of public libraries in the United States, the focus on goodness has been primarily at the input end of the system. Other measures used by library managers fell into the input and process categories, fewer into output, and even fewer (that is, none) into outcome. To a large extent, this is because it is universally easier to measure inputs and processes, and much harder to measure outputs and outcomes. Particularly in service organizations, it is difficult to develop measures of output or outcome, for services are often not tangible, have uncertain and flexible beginning and ending points, and are unclear as to the value received by the user of the service.

Figure 7, the Systems View of the Library in Greater Detail, illustrates the systems model with examples that fit a public library.

In the mid-1970s, some librarians began to do something about this imbalance. The first practical attempt came from DeProspo, Altman, and Beasley. Their *Performance Measures for Public Libraries* (1973) proposed a set of feasible measures of library service. The companion volume (Altman and others 1976), gave detailed instructions for the library wishing to implement the measures. For the first time, libraries had access to the keystone of the planning-and-measurement structure: measures of output. The authors offered the local library a relatively simple way of looking at output and service quality, without the pain of inventing and testing the measures themselves.

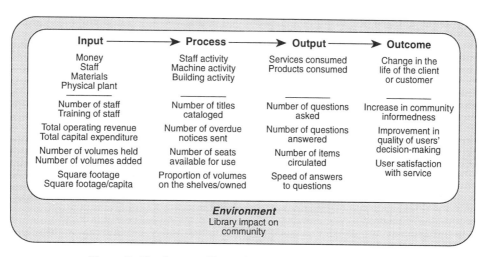

Figure 7. The Systems View of the Library in Greater Detail

DeProspo and others built directly on research that was done at the University of Pennsylvania. That research, by Hamburg and others (1972), sought a single, simple measure of output that reduced the mission and performance of public and academic libraries to their essence, namely, exposing people to recorded information. The resulting measure was an estimate of how much exposure clients were likely to have derived from using a library. It was called "item-use-day."

Hamburg and others succeeded in isolating a single measure, but it was not simple. It did reduce the mission and activities of the library to a universal essence, but the measure was difficult or impossible for most library managers to apply. The Hamburg search for the Grail of Library Goodness did not quite reach its objective.

The DeProspo report was easier to use, but it failed to engage the attention of the average public librarian. The measures and instructions still may have been too complex, and the field may not have been primed sufficiently to adopt the burden of measurement, however simple. But leaders among public library managers were impressed, and 1982 saw a second attempt to create a measurement manual: *Output Measures for Public Libraries (OMPL)* (Zweizig and Rodger 1982). A more readable work, with quite transparent measures, *OMPL* was adopted by many libraries across the country, and the improvements of the second edition (Van House and others 1987) solidified the popularity of the output measures approach to evaluating public library goodness.

OMPL implies that measurement and, ultimately, evaluation are necessary elements in running an effective library. From their wide adoption of it, public library managers seem to agree. By virtue of its emphases—measures of *output*, as opposed to input or processes— *OMPL* implies that service is what matters most.

Twelve years later, *Output Measures for Public Library Service to Children (OMC)* was published (Walter 1992). It parallels *OMPL* to a large extent, while adding data elements that are particular to service to children.

In addition to *OMPL*, other public library measurement efforts are under way. The Public Library Data Service (PLDS) is an annual cumulation and analysis of output measures and other data from a self-selected set of libraries, nationwide (Public Library Association 1990). The output measures of *OMPL*, selected input measures, and occasional special data elements are collected, tabulated, and reported annually. Libraries report their data voluntarily.

In *OMPL* and PLDS, the manager has available a nationally accepted and reported set of measures of output of public libraries, some innovative, some traditional. *OMPL* adds to the perennial output measure, circulation, such others as Reference Fill Rate, Author/Title Fill Rate, and In-Library Use, providing a more nearly complete depiction of how the library touches its users. Public libraries can now paint a more detailed picture of what the library produces from its inputs, or resources—a more accurate assessment of how much the community is getting for its tax dollar. The result is a more balanced assessment of the system called library. On the specific topic of service to youth, *OMC* promises the same advancement in measurement and may come to enjoy the same wide acceptance.

A recent enterprise, the Federal-State Cooperative Data Service (FSCS), coordinates the collection of public library data at the state and the national levels. The data elements (measures) are traditional ones, emphasizing inputs and processes, such as "Public Service Hours Per Week" and "FTE Employees" (Task Force 1989).

In FSCS, the public library manager has a national reporting network for traditional input and process data on libraries. The FSCS system promises to deliver data on almost the total census of public libraries in the United States, and to do it in a timely manner.

Important parts of the goodness question—quantitative and, to a lesser degree, qualitative assessment of selected outputs—have been answered. But many remain.

As public library managers become accustomed to using output measures, thanks to *OMPL,* many see a need for more and different measures that reflect other aspects of the library, that reflect local objectives, needs, and criteria more directly, and that speak more directly to local decision-makers and stakeholders.

Planning

Setting strategic direction for an organization—also known as long-range planning, strategic planning, and "comprehensive rational planning" (Molz 1990)—has become increasingly important in organizations of all types and has been a driving concern among many public library managers for nearly two decades.

The purpose of strategic planning is to direct an organization successfully into the future—to determine its mission, goals, and objectives, or a "vision of success" (Bryson 1988) and to establish the means by which it will get there. The process and the resulting document (the plan) direct the organization's behavior. And then the organization's effectiveness is judged by comparing its accomplishments with its plan: "Did we achieve what we planned? How effective are we, in terms of our vision?"

The formal planning process is the means by which the organization (1) sets its direction for the future, (2) establishes the criteria by which it will judge itself, and (3) designs the actions needed to succeed.

In the planning process, evaluation of organizational effectiveness is ultimately a question of how well the organization matches its vision of success. Certain products of formal planning can be used in evaluating the organization's effec-

tiveness more explicitly, namely, objectives. Objectives contain explicit criteria against which evaluations can be made. In the ideal, they are based on quantitative measures (for instance, "register x% of the adult population"). With quantitative measures, the degree of success in achieving an objective—that is, goodness—can be assessed unambiguously. The organization's strategies may be altered if they prove not to be successful, as determined by looking at the objectives and measures together.

The first planning manual for public librarians grew directly out of the localization movement among the public library leadership. *A Planning Process for Public Libraries* (Palmour, Bellasai, and DeWath) appeared in 1980. It was revised substantially and reincarnated in *Planning and Role Setting for Public Libraries* (PRSPL— McClure and others 1987). *PRSPL* provides guidance in assessing community needs for public library service; offers a set of standard roles from which a public library might choose in building its broad statement of mission; and takes the reader through the steps of a formal strategic planning process. The second edition of the measures volume, *OMPL,* is explicitly linked to the planning manual, to form a coordinated set of recipes for planning and measurement.

Planning and Evaluation

The two manuals approach planning and measurement in a traditional way and are based on some standard assumptions:

First, that the library can identify a unified set of goals and objectives that are to be optimized.

Second, that there is sufficient constancy in the library and its environment for long-term planning to make sense.

Third, that the library can identify and measure at least its major outputs.

Fourth, that decisions about resource allocation are made at least in part rationally, based on data.

Fifth, that the library has some control over its outputs and outcomes.

Sixth, that the evaluation system affects decisions about the library's direction, objectives, and strategies. What the organization knows and pays attention to shapes the judgments and choices that are made.

Seventh, that planning and measurement depend to some degree on the political process, which involves multiple stake-holder groups.

Any management tool can be misused if applied too zealously, without regard for its limits. In the last ten years or so, a number of respected management analysts have criticized formal goals-based planning in one respect or another, and have proposed alternatives (Molz 1990). One of the most eminent writers, Mintzberg (1989), warns against monolithic devotion to formal strategic planning. He claims that it is analytic rather than synthetic, that it "decomposes" the broad direction of the organization into specific objectives and particular means for achieving them—usually evaluated using hard data—and that, therefore, it tends to produce "incremental adaptations rather than innovative breakthroughs" (Mintzberg 1989, 72). It shows a concern for the trees rather than the forest. The result can be an organizational agenda that is rigid, detailed, and unimaginative; often correct, in the micro and wrong in the macro aspects of the organization's management.

Mintzberg proposes an additional type of direction-setting, one which permits "synthesis" of the organization's strengths with environmental realities and which allows intuition, creativity, and inspiration in the planning process. He claims that this format is more likely to result in innovative direction for the organization. Moreover, he says that both the *synthetic* and *analytic* approaches are necessary—the former to achieve Bryson's vision of success, the latter to control activity in the direction of that vision.

What are the implications of all this for assessing and communicating library effectiveness?

- That the organization cannot substitute analysis for a good vision of success.
- That the library's method of representing itself must speak to both the vision and the specific objectives and strategies by which the library achieves the vision.
- That innovation may well arise from unexpected information about the library's performance, its users, or its community and environment.
- That the planning process itself generates a need for added information, as questions arise about how well the library is doing.
- That the planning process results, in part, in the design of the library's evaluation system: The goals and objectives define the criteria and measures by which some evaluation takes place.

- And vice versa, that the evaluation system directs decision-makers' attention and helps them define the goals and objectives.
- That the ability of data to reflect organizational reality is limited. Therefore, evaluation cannot be restricted to quantifiable information. The complete picture requires a multitude of representations, information that is both quantitative and qualitative, and information that tells how successful the library is in achieving a particular objective (for instance, increasing usership by 20 percent) as well as achieving a general vision (for instance, becoming a valued gateway to information for municipal officials). Both data and stories will be required to paint the whole library picture.

Budgeting

Budgets are an essential way of representing an organization's effectiveness. Although the budget, strictly speaking, is a projection of the library's economic future—a contract for spending—it becomes a report of expenditures, in retrospect, a *record* of past spending. The record provides funders and governors of the service with information about the return on their investment (goodness achieved) for making comparisons across organizational units or cost centers.

The simplest budget format is the lump-sum, or memo-type, budget. It consists simply of allocating an amount of money to an activity (organization), with no specification as to how or why the money is to be spent. This form of budget simply asserts that the organization will spend an allocation of money. Many assumptions are embedded in this approach: that the organization is producing the right products or services; that it is doing so with acceptable efficiency; that it addresses the right markets; and that it reaches the right customers in sufficient numbers. In short, that it is good. (A contrasting assumption is that even more complex budgeting systems do not adequately account for expenditures and outputs and that this approach is adopted out of despair for all others.)

In fact, the weakness of the lump-sum budget in controlling and representing goodness is why most organizations, including libraries, have abandoned such a budget format for more complex ones.

The drive toward greater accountability in organizations requires a sharper representation of effectiveness and has led to budgeting innovations. Formats have evolved to express the organization's effectiveness more completely. The new formats have allowed the budget to grow from an instrument that dwelt single-mindedly on inputs to one that includes outputs. A budget can now make statements about the transformation of input (resource) to output (consumed service), not just the consumption of input. Greater accountability of the organization is the goal. Some proposed formats—although extremely difficult to implement—have blended elements of strategic planning, evaluating, and costing into a mighty management machine that integrates goals, costs, outputs, and measures of service. Such budget formats are complex instruments of planning and control.

The *line-item budget*, the most common format, shows the *costs* of specific input categories or items, such as staff salaries and benefits, supplies, operation of the physical plant, library materials, and the like. The line-item budget specifies budgetary *inputs* to the organization, but shows no relationship to the processes within the organization or to its outputs. It presents expenditures more finely than the lump-sum budget. And it is possible to use the information in more interesting ways—for instance, comparing materials expenditure and staff expenditure. Still, it specifies nothing other than inputs.

The *program budget* shows the costs of broad *programs* of activity, such as technical services, circulation, reference, administrative services, or public relations. It attempts to link input (money spent) to process (organizational activity) so that budgeting is more closely tied to the organization's functioning.

The *performance budget* displays the costs of broad programs of activity as well as the levels of program *performance* to be achieved during the budget period—for instance, "process 3,000 new titles during the year" and "handle 10,000 reference questions per reference librarian during the year." Performance levels are specified for each program of activity, which may be either internal processes or products (outputs) of the library.

The *Planning, Programming, and Budgeting System* (PPBS) incorporates *objectives*—particularly product/service objectives—of the organization, linked to *alternative means* of achieving the objectives, to *measures* by which to evaluate the degree of success in achieving the objectives, and, of course, to *costs* of achieving the objectives. This complex form of budgeting brings output objectives, measures, money, and aspects of strategic planning (objectives and alternatives, especially) together. The effectiveness picture that PPBS paints is primarily one of benefit-for-cost—how much benefit is received for what cost. The complexity of this budget format, the expense of honoring all of its requirements, and the need to be almost spiritually in tune with its premise and all of its interlocking elements caused it to collapse from its own weight. Not many years after PPBS's adoption as the federal government's budgeting bible, it was abandoned (Molz 1990). Few organizations use it today.

The *zero-based budget* (ZBB) shows program bundles, *alternative possible levels of program achievement*, and the related costs. In essence, ZBB offers (1) *alternative* levels of effectiveness and of funding to the funding authorities and (2) when last year's spending and accomplishments are reviewed, a *comparison* of actual effectiveness in each program area to the levels of effectiveness that might have been achieved with less, or more, funding. Some variations on ZBB have included performance measures.

As it did to most life forms, evolution made the simple budget format complex. ZBB is so complex that very few libraries, if any, use it in its full form, if we can assume that a sample of 15 libraries in the mid-80s is still somewhat representative today (Koenig and Alperin 1985). But we could speculate from the same data that a number of libraries are probably using some modification of it today—perhaps as many as one-third, according to that study. PPBS is even more complex, and its extinction seems even more certain, perhaps a fait accompli. Koenig and Alperin indicated that none of the 15 libraries had even tried it. Used or not, the two formats show how budgeting mechanisms have been invented to give more complete representations of effectiveness.

In a recent best-selling book, Osborne and Gaebler (1992) describe several entrepreneurial alternatives to budgeting. They are offered as improvements on most current public-sector budgeting methods which, according to Osborne and Gaebler, are not tied to results and encourage waste (particularly the spend-it-or-lose-it rule common to most public budgets). A summary of Osborne's and Gaebler's alternatives follows.

1. Mission-driven budgeting eliminates line items, minimizes rules, and maximizes flexibility. In its simplest manifestation, budgets

are formula-driven. Each department gets last year's appropriation, with an increment for inflation and population growth. Money that isn't spent by the end of the fiscal year can be kept, giving units an incentive to save money and the resources to test new ideas and respond to changing circumstances.

2. Output budgeting focuses on outputs of services. It defines and measures mission and outputs. Funding may or may not be tied directly to output volume. When it is, legislators base their decisions on the levels of service that they want to achieve.

3. Outcome budgeting focuses on quality of outcome of services produced, not just volume. Outcome is measured; funding may or may not be tied to the levels and quality of outcome achieved. When it is, again legislators base their decisions on the levels of service that they want to achieve.

4. Customer-driven budgeting puts control of the budget in the hands of the consumer through vouchers, cash grants, and funding systems that allocate a dollar amount for each person served.

The authors discuss the circumstances under which each of these approaches may or may not be appropriate, and their strengths and limitations. What is important is that each of these approaches, like the "evolved" budget forms discussed earlier, is an attempt to connect more closely the funds expended and the results achieved, and in addition seeks to create incentives for public organizations to maximize the yield on their expenditures.

Budget formats have evolved from input- to output-oriented, from simple statements of resource to be expended toward statements complex enough "to inspire rational choices from among alternative courses of action" (Molz 1990, 48). To this extent, the latter-day formats result in richer statements about an organization's effectiveness. Budgeting is a political process, and the newer budgeting formats are intended to represent the organization's effectiveness more comprehensively, showing at the same time the relationship between input, process, output/outcome, and the environment (Wildavsky 1968).

All of these more complex methods are aimed at clarifying for decision-makers the services or outputs that they are "buying" with budget allocations. In doing so, they highlight the need to define and measure the organization's effectiveness to ensure that it is producing the right outputs and maximizing the yield from its resources.

Appraising Individual Performance

Even libraries that don't appraise organization-level effectiveness generally do appraise individual performance, as a result of the growing legal complexities of the entire area of personnel. Performance appraisal addresses individual rather than organizational effectiveness. In its more contemporary forms, performance appraisal parallels at the individual level some aspects of organization-level strategic planning and measurement. Thus, it also deals with effectiveness. Two methods are especially worth mention: MBO and BARS.

Management by Objectives (MBO) is a method of directing individual effort and assessing individual effectiveness against explicit performance objectives and measures of achievement. It is parallel in these respects to formal strategic planning. In its simplest form, it amounts to periodic discussions between employee and employer in which employee performance is evaluated against concrete, often quantified, objectives (e.g., "make 600 students library-literate in six months") and new objectives are set for the next evaluation period. MBO is focused on the employee's "output" effectiveness—the extent to which the employee has performed effectively—and emphasizes results rather than effort.

Although MBO is not being used, per se, by many library organizations (Molz 1990), it has influenced personnel practice in many libraries as well as other public sector organizations because of its emphasis on specific employee achievement.

An alternative to MBO is the behaviorally anchored rating scale (BARS), a more recent invention. In part, BARS arose because achievement of *effect* in many areas is difficult to assess. For instance, one can easily count the number of students a librarian instructs in library skills, but it is more difficult to assess the degree to which skills were learned. In such a case, one may turn to BARS, wherein the employee's *behaviors*, rather than *achievement*, are assessed—such as the number of people given bibliographic instruction or, in the reference function, the employee's number of questions answered, manner of interaction with the user, skill at negotiating a question, and so forth. BARS is focused on the employee's "processes."

In many organizations, especially public sector organizations—including public libraries—it may be desirable to use both methods in combination. One would appraise the achievement of actual output where possible and, lacking that, the achievement of desirable behaviors. Schneier and Beatty (1979) offer a means for merging the two performance appraisal methods. The view of individual effectiveness is not clearly focused on one aspect or another, but on a mixture: behaviors here, outputs there. There is an acknowledged unevenness in such an appraisal. The caution, when talking about *organization-level effectiveness*, is that it is not equatable with individual effectiveness. Summing up individual employee effectiveness does not necessarily offer an accurate picture of organization effectiveness. Conceivably, an organization with employees appraised as effective could be, as a whole, ineffective—the employees doing good jobs individually, but the wrong jobs in terms of what the customer needs or wants.

Conclusion

A number of management tools have been developed to help libraries assess and represent their effectiveness. The most notable are *Planning and Role Setting for Public Libraries* and *Output Measures for Public Libraries*, which have been widely adopted. These both take a goal-based approach, which, as we have seen, is only one of several possible approaches, and imply a set of assumptions about decision-making that may not always hold.

Related management tools include budgeting and performance evaluation. Both are used to assess and control organizational performance, and for each a variety of methods has been proposed that can describe to varying degrees the library's effectiveness.

Underlying each of these tools is the general systems model that assumes that the organization can define effectiveness, assess its effectiveness, and then make the needed course corrections to use its resources to even greater effect. A critical component of this model of decision-making is that the various levels of decision-makers can define their goals (and agree on those goals) and that they have adequate information to assess the organization and make decisions.

This is relatively easy (perhaps not easy, but *relatively* easy) when an organization has a limited set of decision-makers to be concerned about and produces a clear product. It is more difficult when the organization is in the public sector, with a complex array of stakeholders, and when the organization's goals are unclear and multiple and its products intangible and transitory.

The next chapter looks at the nature of the public library and defining and assessing its effectiveness.

References

Altman, Ellen, Ernest R. DeProspo, Philip M. Clark, and Ellen Connor Clark. 1976. *A Data Gathering and Instructional Manual for Performance Measures in Public Libraries.* Chicago: Celadon Press.

Bryson, John M. 1988. *Strategy Planning for Public and Nonprofit Organizations.* San Francisco: Jossey Bass.

Buckland, Michael K. 1988. *Library Services in Theory and Context,* 2nd ed. New York: Pergamon.

DeProspo, Ernest R., Ellen Altman, and Kenneth E. Beasley. 1973. *Performance Measures for Public Libraries.* Chicago: American Library Association.

Hamburg, Morris, Richard C. Clelland, Michael R. W. Bommer, Leonard E. Ramist, and Ronald M. Whitfield. 1974. *Library Planning and Decision-Making Systems.* Cambridge, Mass.: MIT Press.

Koenig, Michael E. D., and Vistor Alperin. 1985. "ZBB and PPBS: What's Left Now That the Trendiness Has Gone?" *Drexel Library Quarterly* 21 (Summer): 19–38.

McClure, Charles R., Amy Owen, Douglas L. Zweizig, Mary Jo Lynch, and Nancy A. Van House. 1987. *Planning and Role Setting for Public Libraries.* Chicago: American Library Association.

Minimum Standards for Public Library Systems, 1966. 1967. Chicago: American Library Association, Public Library Association, Standards Committee.

Mintzberg, Henry. 1989. *Mintzberg on Management: Inside Our Strange World of Organizations.* New York: Free Press.

Molz, Redmond Kathleen. 1990. *Library Planning and Policy Making: The Legacy of the Public and Private Sectors.* Metuchen, N.J.: Scarecrow Press.

Osborne, David, and Ted Gaebler. 1992. *Reinventing Government: How the Entrepreneurial Spirit Is Transforming the Public Sector.* Reading, Mass.: Addison-Wesley.

Palmour, Vernon E., Marcia C. Bellassai, and Nancy V. DeWath. 1980. *A Planning Process for Public Libraries.* Chicago: American Library Association.

Public Library Data Service Statistical Report, '90. Annual. Chicago: Public Library Association.

Schneier, Craig E., and Richard W. Beatty. 1979. "Combining BARS and MBO: Using an Appraisal System to Diagnose Performance Problems." *The Personnel Administrator* 24 (September): 51–60.

Task Force on Federal-State Cooperative System for Public Library Data. 1989. *An Action Plan for a Federal-State Cooperative System for Public Library Data.* Washington, D.C.: U.S. National Commission on Libraries and Information Science; National Center for Education Statistics.

Van House, Nancy A., Mary Jo Lynch, Charles R. McClure, Douglas L. Zweizig, and Eleanor Jo Rodger. 1987. *Output Measures for Public Libraries,* 2nd ed. Chicago: American Library Association.

Walter, Virginia. 1992. *Output Measures for Public Library Service to Children.* Chicago: American Library Association.

Wildavsky, Aaron. 1968. "Budgeting as a Political Process." *International Encyclopaedia of the Social Sciences,* vol. 2. Macmillan and Free Press.

Zweizig, Douglas L., and Eleanor Jo Rodger. 1982. *Output Measures for Public Libraries.* Chicago: American Library Association.

The Nature of the Library Organization and Implications for Effectiveness

Being an analysis of what makes the public library organization tick in its environment—how it lives and changes and the elements that determine its goodness.

The discussion up to this point has been about effectiveness in fairly general terms and about the tools that libraries have used to monitor and improve their effectiveness. The purpose of this chapter is to look more closely at the characteristics of the public library and what they imply for the processes of monitoring and presenting the library's effectiveness.

The Nature of the Library

Effectiveness is a shifting concept, the definition and presentation of which are largely dependent on political, social, and economic contexts. A large number of stakeholders contribute to decision-making about the library. Their preferences about the library's various features (physical plant, resources, staff, services, community impact, and so on) and their assessment are critical. The rational, goal-maximizing concept of effectiveness that underlies the tools described in chapter 2 is useful, especially in representing achievement of expressed goals; but it is a limited view of effectiveness, especially in light of these characteristics:

- The library is publicly funded.
- The library produces services (not goods).
- Library use is largely self-service.

The Library as a Public Organization

Osborne and Gaebler (1992) identify many of the problems inherent in measuring results in the public sector. They offer the following precepts for performance measurement in the public sector (pp. 146–54):

- What gets measured gets done.
- If you don't measure results, you can't tell success from failure.
- If you can't see success, you can't reward it.
- If you can't reward success, you're probably rewarding failure.
- If you can't see success, you can't learn from it.
- If you can't recognize failure, you can't correct it.
- If you can demonstrate results, you can win public support.

A number of features of public sector organizations make assessing and presenting effectiveness both important and problematical:

1. *Revenues and outputs are separated*. In public sector organizations, revenues are separated from delivery of service. The taxpayers and the decision-makers who mandate and oversee the library are not necessarily those who benefit from the library. Library management shares many major decisions with people outside the library (Heymann 1987), some of whom are genuinely concerned about the library, some of whom are not. Representing the library's effectiveness, then, is critical because revenues depend on political decision-makers, not consumers.

2. *A common metric is lacking*. Public-sector organizations generally lack an agreed-upon bottom line by which they are to be evaluated, such as (in the private sector) net profits or return on investment. The more vague the goals and the more difficult the outputs and outcomes are to identify and measure, the more difficult it is to choose how to rep-

resent the library and identify a basis for evaluation.

3. *The decision-making process is bigger than the library.* Decisions about public library funding are made within a larger context. The political process consists of interest groups, power, and log-rolling. The library's budget is just one of a series of decisions that the key players make, as they come together again and again for budget and policy decisions. They develop a continuing relationship. The process is somewhat like a courtroom where the judge, prosecutor, and defense attorney see one another in court repeatedly while the defendant—supposedly the most important person there—is just passing through. The library is just one of many local services addressed in the decision-making process, and it can easily be an alien presence.

4. *The library has neither foes nor champions.* The library is what Wilson (1989) terms a majoritarian bureaucracy: few citizens actively work either for or against it. The library costs each taxpayer relatively little, so few work to avoid or reduce library costs. The benefits of the library for most individuals are also relatively small, so people rarely work to acquire them. Schools offer a contrasting example: many parents are willing to invest considerable time and effort to ensure that their children get good schooling. And the size of the school taxes gives at least some taxpayers sufficient incentive to monitor school performance and spending.

Although library support (and opposition) may be mobilized on particular decisions, the library does not have a readily identifiable, ongoing constituency operating within the political sphere on a regular basis. The closest is the library friends group. Such groups can provide economic support, such as fund-raising and volunteer service, on a continuing basis. However, they tend to mobilize politically only in crises, which reduces their effectiveness because they are not part of the ongoing political process. In contrast, interest groups that play an active role in decisions about many government services are more powerful, in part, because they use their influence repeatedly, on a number of issues. Decision-makers are more likely to worry about taking a stand that incites their opposition.

On the positive side, the public library field can point to examples where external advocacy has been cultivated. Tulsa is one instance where the director has forged an ongoing political and fiscal alliance with the power elite of the community (Robbins and Zweizig 1992).

5. *Library benefits are not widely self-evident.* The public library may be at an added disadvantage because its value may be less self-evident than that of public services that obviously address pressing social needs: when the water supply or trash collection is being threatened, how willing are politicians to support a library, whose benefits are diffuse or uncertain?

The Service Organization

Libraries share with other service organizations several characteristics that affect the assessment and presentation of their effectiveness. The most notable characteristics are the intangibility of their outputs, the face-to-face quality of much service delivery, and uncertainty about cause and effect.

1. *Intangibility.* Service organizations produce services rather than goods. Service is intangible. That is, it cannot always be easily observed or stored. The library consists, in a sense, of readiness to serve. Until someone uses the library's resources, no service is produced. And when service does take place—whether employee-delivered or self-service—there is not always a trace left to be observed and counted. Book circulation, which is easily measured, is only part of library use; in-house use of library facilities and materials, and consultation with the staff, are harder to capture.

2. *Partnership between staff and client.* Direct personal contact between staff and client is required for many services. When the individual employee interacts directly with the client, both the employee and the user are critical to the nature and quality of service provided. From the employee side, the service delivered depends on instantaneous decisions: What does this client need? What should I do? How far should I go?

From the client side, the information exchanged between employee and client is the fundamental raw material of any service interaction (Mills 1986). The client communicates his or her need, assesses the appropriateness of the service provided, and determines when the transaction is terminated. The library employee's ability to help is circumscribed by the user's ability and willingness to work with the staff member in translating his or her need into something the library can respond to.

3. *Indeterminant technology.* A third characteristic of libraries as service organizations is frequent uncertainty about the best way to do things. It is often difficult to link cause and effect, inputs, processes, outputs, and outcomes. This characteristic is called indeterminant technology and is common in professional service, which depends on the individual application of judgment to each case that comes to hand.

Technology, in this sense, is the combination of know-how, processes, and resources used to create services. When technology is determinant, it is easy to specify what the organization must do to deliver good service. Organizations like McDonald's rely on determinant technology to control the quality of the product delivered across thousands of service outlets.

The more customized the service required, and the less we know about the links between activities and outcomes, the greater the reliance on the individual employee's efforts and judgment. Checking out books relies on determinant technology. Selecting materials uses indeterminant technology; ordering them uses determinant technology. Answering reference questions can be highly indeterminant.

4. *Observing only the observable.* Our understanding of the links between library services and outcomes (as opposed to outputs) is even less complete. Outcomes take place later, often much later, and outside the library, as the person acts on the information or is changed in some way as a result of the library use. Children's use of the public library helps them do better in the learning process, librarians assume. But how can that be assessed? How can the library measure its role in the child's learning? Which kinds of materials and services have the greatest impact? Who are the most effective staff members, and why? Does any of this vary among different groups of children?

Managing and evaluating employee and organizational performance are complex when the service transaction is difficult to observe and to control. The monitoring of service quality may often be done only on an intermittent, obtrusive basis. Many of the measures in *Output Measures for Public Libraries* (Van House and others 1987), for example, rely on reports from users or staff; others rely on sampling. In many libraries, assessment of service quality (as opposed to quantity) is based more on client complaints than on any systematic assessment.

What is most observable in service organizations is not outputs and outcomes so much as processes. Management may not know what people accomplish, but it does know what they are doing. The processes that can be observed are primarily those performed by the staff and, to a lesser degree, by the clientele. When processes and outputs are observed but outcomes are not, the organization often becomes what Wilson (1989) has termed a procedural organization. The emphasis is on how people do their jobs and further, on the observable parts of their jobs—that is, are they following established procedures?

Evaluation of service organizations such as libraries, therefore, often emphasizes the organizations' processes and their observable outputs, on the assumption that the result is effective outputs and *outcomes.* More generally, evaluation addresses that which is observable with the hope that it correlates with that which is important, but not observable.

Self-Service

Library use is largely self-service. D'Elia and Rodger (1991) found, for example, that fewer than half (42 percent) of the users of the Free Library of Philadelphia asked a librarian for assistance. Often, the only contact with the staff is at the circulation desk; the rest of the user's visit amounts to self-service. Present in many services, such as automated tellers and self-service gas stations, this concept is termed coproduction: The user helps to produce his or her own service.

Advances in information technology are increasing the range of activities that users can perform for themselves. CD-ROMS, for example, allow the user to do the kind of bibliographic searching that used to be limited to the staff.

Unfortunately, many library users fail when

working on their own, or at least aren't as successful as they could have been had they been more expert or made more use of staff. This is the case with traditional services, and may be even more so with advanced information resources.

Self-service limits both the library's ability to serve and its ability to assess and represent its service. Outputs are even more difficult to assess when they are self-service. The only directly observable outputs are those that involve a library process, such as circulation. How does the library know whether users found what they were looking for? Were the things found what they actually needed? Could the library have done more to help? Could the users have done a better job? Assessment of such performance factors is difficult.

The critical role of the library user in library services—as a participant in the face-to-face service transactions and in self-service—further complicates the control and assessment of service quality. The outputs and outcomes of library use are a function of both the library and the user. It may be difficult to separate the contribution of each and to evaluate the library's performance.

Conclusion

As a publicly supported organization, the library depends for its resources on the political process, not on direct assessment by its users. The political process is large and complex, embracing a much broader agenda than just the library's funding, and with a large and varied set of players. The public library is often at a disadvantage in this process because it rarely generates strong feelings among regular participants in the budget process.

The library has to figure out how to explain its mission and persuasively illustrate its excellence. It is hampered in this by the nature of its services: intangible and fleeting and, therefore, difficult to count and evaluate. The library is also highly dependent on the user as a participant in the service transaction, making cross-organizational comparison especially tricky (for example, circulation is much easier for the library to generate in more educated communities than in less educated ones). And, finally, the connection between library operations and outputs and community outcomes is delayed, indirect, and difficult to describe. What has the library done for children at risk in this community? Where would they be without the library?

References

D'Elia, George, and Eleanor Jo Rodger. 1991. *Free Library of Philadelphia Patron Survey: Final Report.* Philadelphia: Free Library of Philadelphia.

Heymann, Philip B. 1987. *Politics of Public Management.* New Haven, Conn.: Yale University Press.

Mills, Peter K. 1986. *Managing Service Industries: Organizational Practices in a Postindustrial Economy.* Cambridge, Mass.: Ballinger.

Osborne, David, and Ted Gaebler. 1992. *Reinventing Government: How the Entrepreneurial Spirit Is Transforming the Public Sector.* Reading, Mass.: Addison-Wesley.

Robbins, Jane B., and Douglas L. Zweizig. 1992. *Keeping the Book$: Public Library Financial Practices.* Fort Atkinson, Wis.: Highsmith Press.

Van House, Nancy A., Mary Jo Lynch, Charles R. McClure, Douglas L. Zweizig, and Eleanor Jo Rodger. 1987. *Output Measures for Public Libraries,* 2nd ed. Chicago: American Library Association.

Wilson, James Q. 1989. *Bureaucracy: What Government Agencies Do and Why They Do It.* New York: Basic.

The Public Library Effectiveness Study

5

Below, a brief description of the research on which is based a model of public library effectiveness.

A comprehensive framework for representing your library's effectiveness is presented in the next chapter. To some extent, the model and its discussion are based on our experience in evaluating and planning for libraries over many years. To a much larger extent, the model is based on our field research in 1988 to 1990 called the Public Library Effectiveness Study. The study originally appeared in several pieces (Childers and Van House 1989a, b, c; Van House and Childers 1990). The full report of that study, incorporating the original pieces and additional analyses, can be found in *The Public Library Effectiveness Study: The Complete Report* (Van House and Childers 1993), a companion volume to this book.

This chapter capsulizes the Public Library Effectiveness Study and sets the foundation for the model of public library effectiveness.

Purpose

The Public Library Effectiveness Study was undertaken to define effectiveness for the U.S. public library, to answer the question, "What are the characteristics of an effective public library?" Its purpose was not to identify effective libraries, but to identify the features that people look for in assessing a library's effectiveness— *the indicators of effectiveness*.

Method

The study employed a series of interviews with selected library stakeholders in five communities on the east and west coasts, followed by a national survey of nearly 2,500 people representing seven library stakeholders groups: library managers, library service staff, members of friends groups, trustees, users, local government officials, and community leaders.

Each respondent was asked to state how important it would be to know about a given item (indicator) if he or she had to describe the effectiveness of his or her library to a peer. Sixty-one indicators were culled from the literature and interviews and collapsed from 257 specific items. The intention was to identify the value attached to each indicator, so as to prioritize the list for public libraries, generally, not to evaluate a particular public library.

Findings

Indicators of Effectiveness

The study generated a comprehensive list of indicators of library effectiveness, ranked and classified so as to indicate how the various constituents, together or separately, view the public library—that is, which indicators they prefer to look at when they assess the goodness of the public library institution. In addition to the 61 indicators on the questionnaire, respondents were asked to add any indicators they thought were missing. Thus, a 62nd indicator, Political and Fiscal (External) Viability of the Library, was uncovered as potentially important. It was written in by 2.5 percent of the total respondents— about 60 people. Had it been suggested on the questionnaire, it is safe to assume that many respondents would have rated it highly.

Differences among Stakeholders

One of the most interesting results of the survey is that the seven stakeholder groups, rather than having very dissimilar views of the public library, tend to have relatively similar views. They tend to look at the same things in assessing public library goodness, rather than different things. That the survey instrument finds only subtle differences across groups may be a function of the instrument and of survey research methods generally. Qualitative research methods such as in-depth interviews are better able to tease out these kinds of differences. And the interviews did reveal some subtle differences. Furthermore, a close look at the survey data shows differences among the groups in the particular weights they give to each of the indicators. These are discussed further in chapter 7.

Dimensions of Effectiveness

The survey results can be used to look at the broad dimensions of public library effectiveness. Because of their *overall* similarity, data for all stakeholder groups were used to group the effectiveness indicators into sets, or *dimensions*, of effectiveness which are composed of related indicators.

Factor analysis produced the dimensions by grouping together the indicators that were similarly rated by the respondents. Factor analysis—a common statistical technique for condensing massive amounts of data—computes which items in a study (indicators) are most closely correlated—that is, which items (indicators) consistently receive similar ratings by the respondents. If two items receive similar ratings consistently, they are viewed, in factor analysis, to be measuring the same underlying thing. Thus, they belong in the same factor (dimension of library performance).

After the computation of factors, the researcher's job is to name each factor so as to include all items. The ideal is that each factor can be given a name that is simple, excludes no item that has fallen into the factor, and intrudes on the conceptual space of no other factor in the computation.

The researcher can approach factor analysis from several different statistical points of view. This gives the researcher the flexibility to produce several factor solutions from the same data in order to arrive at that best set of factors—"best" depending, in part, on how much of the relationship among variables is accounted for in the factor and, in part, on the interpretability (nameability) of the results.

The groupings produced by the factor analysis generated the "definition" of public library

effectiveness. The public library's effectiveness is defined through the Public Library Effectiveness Study as:

Dimension 1: Traditional Counts of Library Activity
Dimension 2: Internal Processes
Dimension 3: Community Fit
Dimension 4: Access to Materials
Dimension 5: Physical Facilities
Dimension 6: Boundary Spanning
Dimension 7: Service Offerings
Dimension 8: Service to Special Groups

The dimensions and their subordinate indicators are the basis for "A Model of Public Library Effectiveness" (AMPLE) in the next chapter. A fundamental strength of AMPLE is that it is based on data from the field. Now and then, an indicator seems to be out of place in its dimension; however, most of the indicators fit logically under their respective dimensions. The dimensions and their subordinate indicators remain as they appeared in the reports of the research, with only a couple of words changed. They are listed in order of their statistical importance in defining the dimensions, from most to least important.

Dimension 1: Traditional Counts
Use and Users
Number of Visits to Library
Reference Volume
Circulation
Variety of Users
Materials Turnover
Materials Expenditure
Total Expenditures
Program Attendance
In-library Use
Materials Owned
Staff Size
Reference Fill Rate
Staff Expenditures
Equipment Usage
Use of Library Compared to Other   Services/Events

Dimension 1 conjures up measures that have been used for decades in describing public libraries. The measures are not unlike those that might be reported for any public sector operation: the major inputs to the organization, the extent to which its products or services are used, and its broad penetration into the market (population). At the bottom of the list are two indicators that were less tightly linked to the others, both in the study responses and intuitively: Equipment Usage and Use of Library Compared to Other Services/Events, which could not be considered "traditional." They appear in the same dimension because they have similar levels of importance in the respondents' opinions.

```
Dimension 2:  Internal Processes

   Managerial Competence
   Staff Morale
   Staff Quality
   Efficiency of Library Operations
   Written Policies
   Goal Achievement
   Staff Helpfulness
   Safety of Users
   Support of Intellectual Freedom
```

Dimension 2 deals mostly with the internal workings of the library: management and supervision, characteristics of staff, organizational climate, and control of internal activities. Intuitively, Support of Intellectual Freedom and Staff Helpfulness seem not to fit this dimension as well.

```
Dimension 3:  Community Fit

   Community Awareness of Offerings
   Users' Evaluation
   Contribution to Community Well-Being
   Services Suited to the Community
   Public Opinion
   Flexibility of Library Management
   Relations with Community Agencies
   Community Analysis
   Staff Suitability to Community
   Public Relations
   Staff Contact with Users
```

Community Fit contains indicators that speak to the library's relationship to the community it serves.

```
Dimension 4:  Access to Materials

   Information about Other Collections
   Inter-Library Loan
   Cooperation with Other Libraries
   Speed of Service
   Materials Availability
   Extent Services are Free
```

In Dimension 4, materials are the prime focus—materials obtained either from the library's own shelves, or from outside sources. Speed and cost are also aspects of access that easily fit here.

```
Dimension 5:  Physical Facilities

   Building Appeal
   Convenience of Building Location
   Building Easy to Identify
   Parking
   Building Suitability
```

One of the most coherent dimensions is Dimension 5. All indicators focus on one aspect or another of Physical Facilities.

```
Dimension 6:  Boundary Spanning

   Political and Fiscal Viability of the Library
      (Indicator #62, added from write-in
      response)
   Board Activeness
   Voluntary Contributions (Gifts, Money, Time)
   Library Products (Booklists, Guides, etc.)
   Energy Efficiency of Building
   Continuing Education for Staff
   Planning and Evaluation
   Public Involvement in Library Decisions
```

Dimension 6 incorporates indicators that relate to spanning the boundaries between the library and the external environment—boards and volunteers, products that advertise the library's services, public involvement in running the library, planning (which considers interfaces between the library and the outside world), and Continuing Education for Staff (which exposes staff to outside influences). The ill-fitting indicator in this dimension is Energy Efficiency of Building.

```
Dimension 7:  Service Offerings

   Range of Materials
   Range of Services
   Convenience of Hours
   Materials Quality
   Newness of Materials
```

Dimension 7 offers a coherent set of indicators that define broadly the nature and quality of services offered.

```
Dimension 8:  Service to Special Groups

   Handicapped Access
   Special Group Services
```

A small dimension comprised of only two indicators, both of which describe services to groups needing special attention, although Handi-

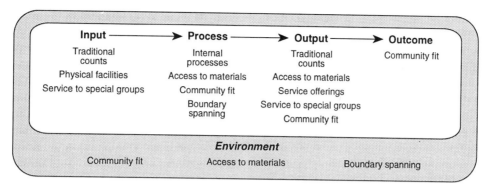

Figure 8. Preference Dimensions Arrayed on the Systems Continuum

Goals	Traditional Counts, Access to Materials, Service to Special Groups
Process	Internal Processes, Service Offerings, Boundary Spanning
Systems Resource	Traditional Counts, Boundary Spanning
Multiple Constituents	Community Fit, Service to Special Groups, Boundary Spanning

Figure 9. Preference Dimensions Compared with the Four Models of Effectiveness

capped Access is far more specific than Special Group Services.

A glance at the indicators listed under the eight dimensions affirms that the model generated by the research is a broad one. When the dimensions are placed under the most related elements of the systems model, as in figure 8—repeating dimensions as the diversity of their indicators calls for it—they cover the continuum. Even at this most general level of analysis, one easily sees that the dimensions range across inputs, processes, and outputs and, by virtue of some of the indicators under the dimension "community fit," even into library outcomes.

One can also compare the dimensions with the four major views of organizational effectiveness. As you will recall from chapter 1, the four major views of organizational effectiveness are:

Goal: The *goal* model views effectiveness in terms of the organization's achievement of specific ends, stressing outputs and productivity, such as consumption of services and proportion of usership.

Process: The *process* model says that organizations are social systems seeking to survive and maintain their equilibrium and that their effectiveness is measured by internal processes and organizational health as well as by goal attainment.

Systems resource: The *systems resource* model emphasizes the organization's need to secure resources from its environment, emphasizing relationships with external resources and their controllers.

Multiple constituencies: The *multiple constituencies* model is concerned with the satisfaction of the organization's various constituent groups, or stakeholders.

In figure 9, where the dimensions are arranged under the four views of effectiveness, it is again clear that the dimensions are wide-ranging. They represent all four of the primary views of organizational effectiveness and affirm the breadth of the model.

References

Childers, Thomas A., and Nancy A. Van House. 1989a. *The Public Library Effectiveness Study: Final Report.* Washington, D.C.: U.S. Department of Education, Office of Educational Research and Improvement.

Childers, Thomas, and Nancy Van House. 1989b. "Dimensions of Public Library Effectiveness." *Library and Information Science Research* 11 (July–September): 273–302.

Childers, Thomas, and Nancy Van House. 1989c. "The Grail of Goodness: The Effective Public

Library." *Library Journal* 114 (October 1): 44–49.

Mills, Peter K. 1986. *Managing Service Industries: Organizational Practices in a Postindustrial Economy.* Cambridge, Mass.: Ballinger.

Osborne, David, and Ted Gaebler. 1992. *Reinventing Government: How the Entrepreneurial Spirit is Transforming the Public Sector.* Reading, Mass.: Addison-Wesley.

Van House, Nancy A., and Thomas Childers. 1993. *The Public Library Effectiveness Study: The Complete Report.* Chicago: American Library Association.

Van House, Nancy A., and Thomas Childers. 1990. "Dimensions of Public Library Effectiveness II: Library Performance." *Library and Information Science Research* 12 (April–June): 131–53.

Van House, Nancy A., Mary Jo Lynch, Charles R. McClure, Douglas L. Zweizig, and Eleanor Jo Rodger. 1987. *Output Measures for Public Libraries*, 2nd ed. Chicago: American Library Association.

Wilson, James Q. 1989. *Bureaucracy: What Government Agencies Do and Why They Do It.* New York: Basic.

A Model of Public Library Effectiveness (AMPLE)

In which is displayed and explicated a framework by which the manager may plan a program of representing the effectiveness of the library.

The Major Uses of AMPLE

In this chapter, the framework that we have alluded to from time to time is unveiled. The framework, or model, is called "A Model of Public Library Effectiveness," or AMPLE. It has three major uses, which focus on the library's program of metrics, or assessment of effectiveness, and on using the metrics to communicate the library's effectiveness to the stakeholders:

- Reviewing your "mix of metrics," your program of assessment;
- Developing a program of assessment; and
- Creating a strategy for communicating to key stakeholders—what to communicate and how.

These can be seen as "steps," all three centering on how the public library represents itself to its various stakeholders. While the printed page requires that the steps be presented in linear order, the reality is that they are all taken at the same time, each step interacting with the others.

In this chapter, we touch briefly on each use of AMPLE to illustrate how the model can be put to use in reviewing your metrics and developing a program of assessment. Creating a communication strategy will be treated at length in chapter 7.

> The use of AMPLE can be broadly indicated, not narrowly prescribed.

Note that the discussion here is indicative, not prescriptive, for it will be the local conditions that prescribe the particulars of applying AMPLE.

Review Your Assessment Program

AMPLE allows you to see how well your assessment program covers all the critical dimensions of the library and the important parts (indicators) that make up those dimensions. The view afforded by the model should tell you how comprehensive the library's assessment program is—whether you have a whole or a partial picture of the library's goodness.

Program assessment operates in two directions: breadth and depth. For breadth, one looks at completeness of coverage *across* the dimensions of AMPLE. For depth, one looks at exhaustive coverage *within* a given dimension. In reviewing depth of library assessment, you may want to focus on the high-ranking indicators and their measures, introduced later as the short AMPLE.

Develop a Program for Assessment

The primary objective of AMPLE is to help the local library develop a considered program for assessment and, ultimately, for communicating the assessment to stakeholders. A more complete and more deliberate assessment should ensue. To reach the point of a full assessment, go in stages: identify what is currently being done, locate the gaps vis-à-vis your local situation, and set an agenda for improved assessment (which tallies to begin; when to develop and apply a checklist or a survey).

A major use of a comprehensive model is to pick and choose the dimensions and indicators that fit the current local situation. It permits the library manager to tune the representation of the library to the need at hand. For instance, if efficiency of operations is of paramount importance to a financially beleaguered county, your library might be wise to give extra weight to indicator 2.8, Efficiency of Library Operations.

Create a Strategy for Communicating with the Stakeholders

The program for assessment is never developed in isolation. It is created with its ends in mind. Indiscriminate collection of data wastes energy. Instead, one considers the reasons for assessment before settling on a measurement program. The primary motivator is to present the organization to a person or group in order to affect their perceptions of, and ultimately behavior toward, the organization.

The facets of creating a strategy for communication are:

- identifying the key stakeholders with whom you are likely to want to communicate on a continuing basis;
- establishing the individual measure(s) that will be most useful in communicating with them; and
- creating the most compelling presentations of the measures for each stakeholder type—formatting the assessment for optimal communication.

The Structure of AMPLE

AMPLE is a hierarchy of dimensions, indicators, and measures, with annotations. The dimensions and indicators were taken directly from the Public Library Effectiveness Study. In trans-

lating the results of the research into something that makes *applied* sense, we adjusted the model produced by the research. First, we did some slight renaming of a dimension; second, we added the 62nd indicator, Political and Fiscal (External) Viability of the Library, written in by enough respondents to convince us that it should not be ignored in the model. Overall, the changes to the research results were minimal. AMPLE is fundamentally the set of dimensions and indicators that was generated by responses from 2,500 people from seven different constituent groups across the country.

The model begins with the *dimensions* derived from the study. It then moves to the next level in the hierarchy, the *indicators*, subordinate terms that define library goodness under each dimension. Finally, it moves to *measures* of those indicators, the means by which the indicators may be described. Figure 10 illustrates these relationships.

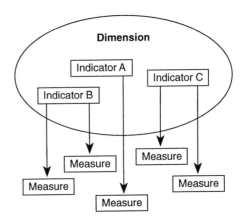

Figure 10. Dimensions, Indicators, and Measures

Figure 11 shows a fragment of AMPLE, illustrating the relationships among dimensions, indicators, and measures as they appear in the model. The full AMPLE begins on page 41.

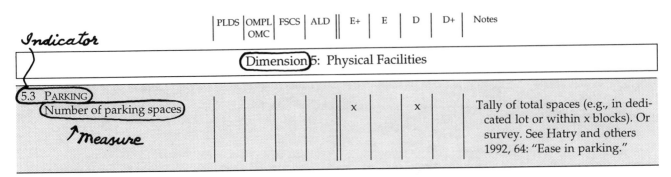

Figure 11. Fragment of AMPLE

The major work on AMPLE beyond the Public Library Effectiveness Study has been to transform the indicators into measures, in order to make AMPLE applicable to a practical library situation. In research language, this is known as "operationalizing" the indicators—turning a concept into a survey question or stating it as a specific data element to collect. AMPLE makes the indicators usable as measures. In identifying measures, we have drawn freely on the last two decades' work on library measurement and evaluation. Our goal is not to create new measures, but to rationalize and systematize the library manager's choice among available measures.

The indicators and measures of AMPLE are based on library services as they were at the time of the study, of course. As new technologies effect changes in library services, new indicators or measures will be required. For instance, electronic access to library documents from home may diminish the usefulness of the indicator "visits to the library" and may require the addition of an indicator related to electronic inquiries, along with an appropriate measure.

The Nature of the AMPLE Measures

For AMPLE, the term "measures" is interpreted freely. Here, measures may be based either on idiosyncratic, personal assessment or on the systematic collection of data. In translating indicators into measures (operationalizing), we have preferred the systematic over the idiosyncratic—for example, a count or an opinion survey—over the opinion of one or a few people, or casual observation. Systematic measures are generally the more difficult of the two to invent locally, but are usually defensible as being more objective and valid. For some indicators, the model offers both systematic and idiosyncratic measures.

Often, one or more measures for a given indicator were turned up in the course of the literature search and interviews of the Public Library Effectiveness Study. They are usually measures that have been used in the field (such as "Number of Users per Capita"), and to some degree this argued for including the measure in AMPLE. From the list of measures thus "affirmed," we selected those that seem to portray each given indicator best and to be most feasible, in terms of data collection, interpretation, and communication.

For some indicators, the literature and interviews suggested no measure. When we could, we invented a measure. The invented measures have not been used or tested, but they are direct reflections of their indicators, carrying a certain amount of face validity. For example, the indicator Staff Contact with Users might lead naturally to such a measure as Number of Professional Contacts with Users, Individual and Group, Inside and Outside the Library. (In some cases you may think that we, in our wisdom, have stretched too much to find a measure. Perhaps we have, preferring to err on the side of "over-operationalizing.")

Some indicators may have no readily available or easily proposed systematic measure—for example, Managerial Competence or Building Easily Identified from the Street. For now, the assessment of library effectiveness in such areas requires idiosyncratic assessment by one or more people in one or more stakeholder groups—library managers, users, citizens, trustees, etc. The assessment may come in the form of statements of one or several individuals' opinions. Or such an idiosyncratic "measure" could be turned systematic by creating, testing, and applying an opinion survey to many people. The results will still be subjective, but more broadly based and offering *systematic* coverage of various opinions.

Many measures may be intuitively obvious, but that doesn't mean that they are easy, or that the manager can escape a certain amount of creativity and invention in using them. Time Spent in Building may require a method of observing user behavior, such as creating a user ticket that is stamped with the time when the user enters and leaves. Number of Formal Groups Served per Annum will require defining your terms ("formal group") and setting your scales for measurement (Do you count groups, or individuals in groups? Do you classify the types of groups? And so on). Services to Populations with Special Needs may require a lengthy assessment by an outside consultant ("idiosyncratic").

To keep the model brief, we eliminated redundancy in the measures as much as possible and, in some cases, left specific decisions about measures to the reader. For instance, measures are rarely given both as a simple frequency (Current Registration, for example) *and* as a per-capita figure (Current Registration per Capita). We chose the form which we thought would be most telling of goodness and assumed the reader would adapt the measure to local needs.

The Short AMPLE

Lest you be daunted, the model uses a gray background to highlight a briefer version, the short AMPLE, with a truncated list of indicators and measures. If the full AMPLE seems too, well, ample, you can choose the short AMPLE.

Appendix A, "The AMPLE Worksheet," also allows you to use either the complete model or just the gray portions as a planning document for your own assessment.

> A brief AMPLE, for the faint of heart and short of time. Look for the gray background.

As shown in the full report of *The Public Library Effectiveness Study* (Van House and Childers 1993), all of the indicators were rated by all stakeholders as at least moderately important in defining public library effectiveness. This is no surprise, because the list was developed from indicators that had already appeared in the literature or in interviews. However, knowing that people who answer questionnaires are inclined toward a positive response, one could assume that the indicators rated at the top of the list are of relatively greater importance and that those at the bottom of the list are of relatively less importance.

Also, collecting data on all indicators is not feasible for most libraries. Therefore, a shorter model of effectiveness is offered. It, like the full AMPLE, is based on the research of the Public Library Effectiveness Study: the indicators rated among the top 31 of the 61 indicators by at least four of the seven stakeholder groups were selected. The 62nd indicator, Political and Fiscal (External) Viability of the Library, was arbitrarily imposed on the short AMPLE, owing to its prominence as a write-in response. Thus, the short AMPLE is a much shorter list, consisting only of the indicators that most stakeholders rated highest—the items that they considered most telling about public library effectiveness.

An interesting thing happens in the short model:

- In the full AMPLE, most of the indicators that reflect *Output Measures for Public Libraries* (Van House and others 1987) are found in the first dimension, "traditional counts." In the short version, only two of these indicators are found. That is, only two of the "traditional counts" were considered top-ranking by most of the stakeholders.
- The sixth dimension, "boundary spanning,"

appears only because we included the write-in indicator, Political and Fiscal (External) Viability of the Library.
- All indicators in the seventh dimension, "service offerings," are included in the short AMPLE.
- A large proportion of the short AMPLE measures are idiosyncratic or depend on opinion survey.
- Service consumption has surprisingly low presence in the short AMPLE. "Number of Visits," "Volume of Reference Questions," and "Contribution to the Well-Being of the Community" are the indicators that most directly suggest contact with the user, or output. The other indicators that come the closest to showing user contact are really service *offerings*, rather than service *consumptions*.

Notes on Using AMPLE

With regard to the *measures:* they are suggestions, rather than prescriptions. If you seek a narrow prescription for your evaluation and communication program, this is not it. AMPLE is a *general* framework to help in creating an assessment and communication program. A certain amount of invention will be needed—for instance, dividing a measure on use into submeasures for adult use and juvenile use, or by format of material used (book, serial, computer, etc.); or creating a survey questionnaire or a trustee checklist.

> For "goodness" sake, don't use AMPLE blindly.

Lest the tail wag the dog, flexibility is needed in using AMPLE, as it is with any model. If your library runs a periodic survey on satisfaction with parking, for example, that measure could readily be used in lieu of the measure "Number of Parking Spaces" (under indicator 5.3, Parking). In many cases, the astute manager will know of locally available measures that will articulate a particular indicator. Good. Use them freely. Using measures that you have used before gives you the added benefit of tracking changes over time.

The Annotated AMPLE

In order to be more useful and usable, each measure in the model is annotated in five ways. Figure 12 demonstrates this.

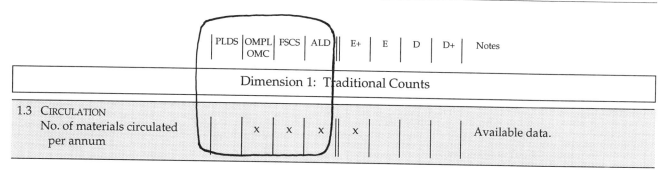

Figure 12. Other Data Collection Efforts in AMPLE

The first annotation: *references to other major data* collection efforts. In the past decade, a number of national efforts to improve the measurement and evaluation of public libraries have been launched. They have aimed at improving the nature of the data collected, the methods used to collect them, and their tabulating and reporting. You may want to emphasize data that have the professional endorsement implied by inclusion in any of the following, in addition to the endorsement implied by the results of the Public Library Effectiveness Study.

- *The Public Library Data Service Statistical Report (PLDS),* which amounts to an annual statistical report of national data from libraries that volunteer to send data in (Public Library Association 1990).
- *Output Measures for Public Libraries (OMPL),* a manual for assessing public library output, also from the Public Library Association (Van House and others 1987). The manual is in use across the country. The measures in the manual are all included in the Public Library Data Service.
- *Output Measures for Public Library Services to Children (OMC),* a manual for assessing outputs for the public library's services to children (Walter 1992). Many of the measures parallel *OMPL* measures; where there is a rel-

evant measure that does not appear in *OMPL,* the notation "*OMC*" appears in the notes column.

- The Federal-State Cooperative System for Public Library Data (FSCS), a project wherein state libraries cooperate with the National Center for Education Statistics in the collection of selected statistics from all U.S. public libraries and their publication in both print and computer form (Task Force 1989).
- The *American Library Directory (ALD),* an annual compilation of statistics about individual public libraries (or systems of libraries). The data are not aggregated (*American Library Directory* 1991).

Figure 12, "Other Data Collection Efforts in AMPLE," illustrates how the model is keyed to the other data collection efforts.

The second annotation: A suggestion as to how *easy or difficult* it would be to take that measure (circled in figure 13), on a four-point scale:

E+ = Easier. Data or knowledge about the measure exists; may require a minor bit of calculation.

E = Easy. Requires data collection or reflection on a qualitative measure—but is relatively simple. Methods of data collection are available or intuitively obvious.

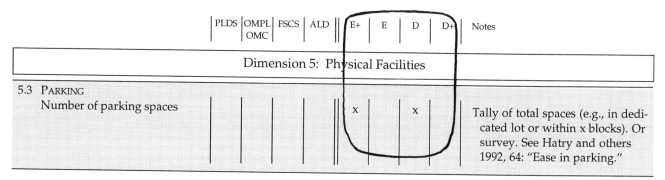

Figure 13. Difficulty of Measures in AMPLE

D = Difficult. Methods are available for data collection, but it will not be easy. Opinion data require an expert's help or considerable exploration of the item.

D+= More Difficult. Methods of data collection or qualitative assessment are not available. Requires local invention or creative synthesis of existing instruments. Inspection (idiosyncratic observation) also falls here, for it is not reliable.

! = Even more difficult than "more difficult." Very time-consuming or conceptually impossible; perhaps not even amenable to idiosyncratic assessment. Labeled "!" under D+.

Generally, the measures done by inspection or tally are easier; the ones done by survey, more difficult.

The third annotation is contained in the "Notes:" An indication of the *type of measure* being proposed (figure 14):

"Tally," a count, such as circulations per capita;

"Inspection," an idiosyncratic observation, such as an expert's opinion; and

"Survey," a systematic observation of opinion or remembered fact, such as a survey of user awareness of library services.

The fourth annotation: *Notes* that clarify and illustrate the measures (figure 15). Where it seemed helpful, we have added brief notes that clarify the brief statement of a measure, clarify the method of collecting data on the measure, or illustrate the measure in some way.

The fifth annotation: *References* to other documents and data collection instruments that offer some guidance for the particular measure (figure 16). In many cases, there are books or articles that will offer advice and counsel when you are faced with a measure that is less than transparent. They may contain a general discussion of the measurement topic, a prototype data collection instrument, or methodological hints. AMPLE includes references to such aids.

Types of Measures in AMPLE

Four broad classes of measure are identified in AMPLE's "Notes."

Available Statistical Data

Every organization has already available a range of data that can be used to describe it. Budgetary data already exist somewhere in the organization.

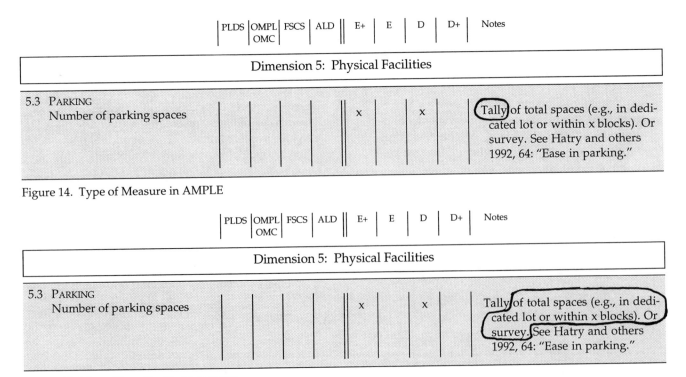

Figure 14. Type of Measure in AMPLE

Figure 15. Notes That Clarify AMPLE Measures

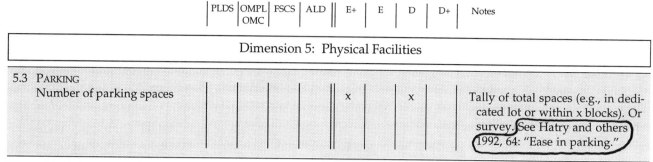

	PLDS	OMPL OMC	FSCS	ALD	E+	E	D	D+	Notes
Dimension 5: Physical Facilities									
5.3 PARKING Number of parking spaces					x		x		Tally of total spaces (e.g., in dedicated lot or within x blocks). Or survey. See Hatry and others 1992, 64: "Ease in parking."

Figure 16. References in AMPLE

You may wish to do further breakdowns for particular purposes, but at least some data already exist. Likewise, some data are produced as by-products of library operations. Virtually every library gets a count of circulation transactions from its circulation system. No additional effort is required to count circulation. Similarly, you may have data on the size of your collection, number of registered borrowers, number of searches of an online catalog, and the like.

Tally

A tally is a quantitative measure: a count of something. Circulation statistics are, of course, tallies of all circulation transactions. The distinction that we want to make here, however, is the effort required of the library staff. Circulation transactions are tallied automatically by the circulation system. We have labeled as "tally" in table 1, "A Model of Public Library Effectiveness," the measures that require tallying activity on the part of the staff.

A tally may be a *census* of all occurrences of a thing, as when we count all reference questions asked during the year. Or it may be a *sample* of the thing, as when we count the number of reference questions asked on a random sample of days in the year. (We often use a sample to then extrapolate to the whole, such as using a sample of reference questions during the year to estimate the annual total.)

One important distinction that affects the level of effort required of a tally is whether it can be done at the convenience of the person doing the tally, or whether it has to be done on a more fixed schedule. Tallies of *things* can be done at the observer's convenience, within certain limits. Tallies of *people's behavior* generally have to be done at the time that the behavior takes place. Counting reference questions, for example, has to be done at the time of the transactions

(notwithstanding the time-honored custom of recording a clutch of reference transactions at the end of a busy period). Tallies that have to be done on a constrained schedule require a higher level of effort than those that are more flexible.

Inspection

The "data" for inspection measures are subjective and idiosyncratic, depending wholly on the experience and opinion of the "inspector," and not on data that are systematically collected. They may consist of the president of the board's opinion as to the competence of the library's management; or—for a rather second-hand opinion—the opinion of the director as to how convenient the users find the library's location. Clearly, a key issue is *who is the inspector*—that is, whose opinions are we using.

We "inspect" where other methods do not exist or are very difficult or impossible to apply (as is the case in evaluating staff morale), or where inspection would be good enough (as in determining the extent of written policies, where their presence or absence is easily and objectively verifiable, and a quantitative measure like "number of pages of written policies" may not be meaningful).

In AMPLE, many inspections can be done fairly casually; but some require deliberate and time-consuming attention. Inspection is an easy method when it consists of asking your own opinion or the opinion of a colleague and that opinion is already formed (for example, "How appealing do you think the users find the building interior?"). It becomes more difficult when one must ask the opinion of someone removed from the library, such as a city personnel officer or an expert on building safety; when one feels compelled to do an informal (nonsystematic) poll, such as asking several users what they think of the library's physical appeal; or when one must give a lot of original thought to the topic or examine existing records to arrive at an opinion (for instance, understanding the library's contribution to the community's education). A formal (systematic) poll of a number of people is no longer inspection, but a survey.

Survey

A survey is the means of systematically asking people about opinions, attitudes, perceptions, behaviors, and remembered facts that are impossible to observe directly, such as experiences of library users. A survey may be conducted face to face, as an interview, or on paper. Generally speaking, a survey generates more valid data than inspection or informal polling, because the questions asked are consistent from person to person and the population is broadly and systematically, rather than arbitrarily, sampled.

Some of the survey items suggested in AMPLE have been tested and are readily available, as is the case in the survey items found in *OMPL* and in survey publications. In many cases, however, the survey item has yet to be created.

Much has been written about surveying, and it is not the purpose of this book to serve as a primer on survey research. However, three common pitfalls of surveys should be heeded. First, many librarians, upon surveying the opinions of library users, have assumed that they have tapped the opinions of the community in general. They are probably wrong. We can't assume that users of a service represent the non-users of the service. Studies of public library users and non-users stretching back 50 years point to many differences among the two groups (for example, Berelson 1949).

Second, in asking people's opinions on the library or any of its features, remember that the public library institution is suffused with the light of a strong halo effect. The public, through their emotional attachment to the public library institution, is very much inclined to view it positively. Even when the library does not give good service—say, fails to yield any of several books

requested—the user is likely to be satisfied with the library in general and even with that day's service. Research has found that, when asking for opinions about any aspect of the library, if that aspect is broken down into its component parts, one is likely to get a more unbiased assessment (D'Elia and Walsh 1983). For instance, rather than asking a user, "Are you satisfied with library reference service?" ask instead specific questions about the response to the last question he or she asked, such as its completeness, its correctness, its speed, the nature of the librarian's greeting, etc.

Having said that, on some occasions, a survey of the public's *feelings* about the public library may be a useful broad gauge of general emotional support and preparedness for, say, a tax referendum.

Third, the information you get depends on the questions asked. If an appropriate question is missing from the questionnaire, the interview schedule, or the observation checklist, it will go unobserved. If it is misstated, it will be misobserved.

Survey of Services

In surveying stakeholders regarding their awareness of particular library services, their use of them, the importance of them, the dollar value of them, or their comparative worth vis-à-vis other services or products, you will need to compile a comprehensive list of library services. In many cases, the list used in a survey will need to include services that are *not* offered, in order to test the true reaction to the library's actual offerings. In preparing such a list, it is difficult to construct one that is internally consistent, with all items at parallel levels of specificity.

Appendix B, "Checklist of Library Services," is a list of candidate library services. It was taken from a study of users, managers, and trustees of Alabama public library services (Kaske, Stephens, and Turner 1986), augmented with a set of reference and information services that we developed independently. Although not exhaustive, the list offers a broad and reasonably parallel set of service options and may inspire you in building your own list.

Table 1. A Model of Public Library Effectiveness

	PLDS	OMPL OMC	FSCS	ALD	E+	E	D	D+	Notes
Dimension 1: Traditional Counts									
1.1 USES AND USERS									
Total uses of all services per annum						x			Tally the uses of all services, including materials, information services, and library facilities.
Current registration per capita		x	x		x				Available data or tally.
Total users per annum per capita							x		Survey of community. Gives a sense of the library's market penetration.
1.2 VISITS TO LIBRARY									
Annual visits (turnstile count)	x	x	x		x	x			Available data. Without a turnstile requires tally of visitors entering.
Frequency of visits per visitor							x		Survey of users.
Time spent in building							x		Survey or observation of users' time in library. See Van House, Weil, and McClure 1990.
Average number of services used during visits							x		Survey. See Van House, Weil, and McClure 1990.
1.3 CIRCULATION									
Number of materials circulated per annum		x	x	x	x				Available data.
. . . and per capita	x	x	x		x				Available data.
Number of materials circulated per person per visit						x			Available data.
Types of materials borrowed per annum					x				Tally (e.g., juvenile materials % of circulation to juvenile % of population; juvenile materials % of circulation to juvenile % of materials budget).
Total materials used		x			x				Available data (circulation) and tally in-library use.
1.4 TOTAL EXPENDITURES									
Total annual expenditure	x		x		x				Available data.
Annual capital expenditure			x		x				Available data.
Annual operating expenditure					x				Available data.
Annual income by source	x		x		x				Such as local, state, federal. Available data.
1.5 REFERENCE VOLUME									
Number of reference transactions per annum	x	x	x		x				Available data or tally.
Patterns of reference usage						x	x		Tally (e.g., by time of day, day of week, season of year; by types of specific service, such as online, manual, instruction, etc.). Survey (e.g., reference transactions per user type).

Table 1. Continued

	PLDS	OMPL OMC	FSCS	ALD	E+	E	D	D+	Notes
1.6 VARIETY OF USERS									
Users (grouped by demographic characteristics)	x					x			E.g., age, gender, income, education, occupation, ethnicity. Public Library Data Service (age only). Survey combined with available data.
as a percentage of total users	x					x			
as a percent of the population in each group	x								
1.7. MATERIALS TURNOVER									
Turnover rate	x	x			x				Available data. Calculate circulation + total volumes.
Turnover rate by type of material		x				x			Same, by format, subject, etc.
1.8 MATERIALS EXPENDITURE									
Materials expenditure per annum	x		x	x	x				Available data.
. . . and + total operating expenditures	x		x		x				Available data.
Materials expenditure by category + total operating operating expenditures					x				By subject, type of material, user type, branch or department, etc. The *American Library Directory* includes expenditure for materials by specific format categories. Available data or tally.
1.9 PROGRAM ATTENDANCE									
Program attendance per annum (audience size)	x	x				x			Tally. In-library programs only.
Attendance at out-of-library programs	x	x				x			Tally. In *OMC* only.
1.10 IN-LIBRARY USE									
In-library use of materials	x	x	x			x			Tally.
. . . and as a % of circulation	x	x	x			x			Tally.
1.11 MATERIALS OWNED Includes book, serial, audio, visual, microform, and computer formats									
Items held	x		x	x	x				Available data or tally. *PLDS:* books and serials only. The *American Library Directory* includes expenditure for materials by specific format categories.
Items by type, as a % of total items					x	x			Available data or tally (e.g., juvenile, adult; format; classification category).
1.12 STAFF SIZE									
Staff size	x		x	x	x				Available data or tally.
Professional staff size per capita					x				Available data or tally.
Number of staff + circulation					x				Available data or tally.
Number of public service staff + users per annum						x			Tally. Easiness of this measure depends on having data on users per annum.
Public service staff per hour open					x				Available data.

Table 1. Continued

	PLDS	OMPL OMC	FSCS	ALD	E+	E	D	D+	Notes
1.13 REFERENCE FILL RATE									
Reference fill rate	x	x				x			Tally.
Correct answers to reference questions							x		Tally. See Lancaster 1988, 111–14, for a concise presentation of an unobtrusive methodology for assessing correctness of answers.
Scope and depth of reference resources					x				Inspection. See appendix B, "Checklist of Library Services."
1.14 STAFF EXPENDITURES									
Expenditure for personnel	x		x	x	x				Available data.
. . . and as % of total expenditures	x		x		x				Available data.
1.15 EQUIPMENT USAGE									
Number of pieces of equipment available, by type						x			Tally (e.g., microfilm, projection, computer, TTY, etc.).
Number of equipment uses						x			Tally.
. . . and per annum						x			Tally.
Percentage of time equipment is in use						x			Tally. See Van House, Weil, and McClure 1990; DeProspo, Altman, and Beasley 1973.
1.16 USE OF LIBRARY COMPARED TO OTHER SERVICES/EVENTS									
Library uses per annum compared to other product or service use						x			Available data (circulation) and calculation (e.g., attendance at sports events, commercial book sales or video rentals, television viewing, etc.).

Dimension 2: Internal Processes

	PLDS	OMPL OMC	FSCS	ALD	E+	E	D	D+	Notes
2.1 MANAGERIAL COMPETENCE									
Managerial competence					x			!	Easily done by inspection. A more valid and more systematic approach would require great effort.
2.2 STAFF MORALE									
Staff morale					x	x			Easily done by inspection. A more valid, but difficult, approach could employ survey instruments used in organization development work.
2.3 STAFF QUALITY									
Overall staff quality					x			!	Easily done by inspection. A more systematic approach requires development of a survey instrument.
Total professionals + total staff					x				Available data.

Table 1. Continued

	PLDS	OMPL OMC	FSCS	ALD	E+	E	D	D+	Notes
2.4 STAFF HELPFULNESS									
Helpful, courteous staff, concerned about client					x			x	Easier by inspection. Hard if a survey is undertaken. See Van House and others 1987; Hatry and others 1992, 59: "Measure 10: Percentage of persons using library who rate helpfulness and general attitude of library staff as satisfactory."
Level of staff assistance to users					x			x	Easier by inspection. Systematic data will require a survey. See also dimension 1, "reference fill rate."
2.5 SUPPORT OF INTELLECTUAL FREEDOM									
Library endorsement of intellectual freedom statements					x				Inspection. Evidence by written policy, resolutions, etc.
Use of materials regardless of content, format, or treatment, by any user					x				Inspection.
2.6 CONTRIBUTION OF LAYOUT, CATALOG, AND SIGNAGE TO SELF-USE (Indicator #63)									
"Transparency" of building layout					x	x			Inspection or survey.
Utility of catalog					x			x	Inspection or survey.
Utility of internal signage					x			x	Inspection or survey.
2.7 GOAL ACHIEVEMENT									
Extent to which formal library objectives are achieved					x				Easier by inspection if quantified objectives exist, if no written goals exist or if objectives require extensive data collection.
2.8 EFFICIENCY OF LIBRARY OPERATIONS									
Operating expenditures per capita	x		x		x				Available data.
Operating expenditures + number of total client uses per annum						x			Available data. Dependent on having uses data.
Number of materials processed +dollars expended on materials processing						x			Available data. May require refiguring budget on information.
Operating expenditures + library activity index or workload level							x		Available data and tally. Requires establishing workload or activity measures.
2.9 WRITTEN POLICIES									
Existence of written policies					x				Inspection (e.g., policies exist for services, fees, and collection development).

Table 1. Continued

	PLDS	OMPL OMC	FSCS	ALD	E+	E	D	D+	Notes
2.10 SAFETY OF USERS Security of users of building, inside and outside					x				Easier by inspection of such safety factors as rating on fire inspections, currency of elevator inspections; or tally of security guards per hours open, safety statistics.

Dimension 3: Community Fit

	PLDS	OMPL OMC	FSCS	ALD	E+	E	D	D+	Notes
3.1 COMMUNITY AWARENESS OF OFFERINGS Community awareness of library services							x		Survey. Use appendix B, "Checklist of Library Services": "Which of the following services does your library/branch provide?"
3.2 USERS' EVALUATION User evaluation of service received . . . immediately upon receiving the service . . . after using the information/ knowledge					x x x	x x x			Survey or informal polling of users. See D'Elia and Walsh 1983; Van House and others 1987, 131, for examples of a user satisfaction survey. Easier by inspection or anecdotal evidence.
3.3 CONTRIBUTION TO COMMUNITY WELL-BEING Contribution of library to community well-being					x			x	Survey of community leaders, comparing library with other services. Easier by informal polling or by inspection, considering, for example, the library as a community symbol or monument to community pride. Inspection.
Contribution of library to individual well-being . . . and to subgroups (e.g., business, students, etc.)								x x	Survey. See King Research, Ltd. 1991, 63, "needs fill rate"; and 21, "purpose of use."
Contribution to education of the community.								x	By focussed informal polling or inspection; or by survey of users.
Return on investment								!	Survey and tally. Community benefits + library operating expenditure. However, there is currently no way of measuring the benefit of the library in a single metric and rendering that into dollars.

Table 1. Continued

	PLDS	OMPL OMC	FSCS	ALD	E+	E	D	D+	Notes
3.4 SERVICES SUITED TO THE COMMUNITY									
Suitedness of services to community					X		X		Easier by inspection. Hard by informal polling.
Extent to which target populations are reached						X	X		Easy through available data and calculation if appropriate demographic data on each user, such as zip code, exist. Difficult if a special survey is required.
3.5 PUBLIC OPINION									
Public opinion of library							X		By survey or informal polling. Can be combined with a community awareness survey.
3.6 FLEXIBILITY OF LIBRARY MANAGEMENT									
Adaptability of the organization and of management						X			By long-term inspection of the library's or management's response to the external environment.
Adoption of innovation, both number and speed							X		Inspection. See Damanpour and Childers 1985 for prototype checklist.
3.7 STAFF SUITED TO THE COMMUNITY									
Demographics of staff compared with demographics of population						X			Tally (e.g., ethnicity, language). Inspection of data.
Ability of staff to serve community						X			Inspection.
3.8 STAFF CONTACT WITH USERS									
Number of contacts between users and service staff						X			Inspection.
Proportion of hours open when staff is available at service points						X			Tally, by systematic observation.
3.9 PUBLIC RELATIONS									
Number of public relations events per annum						X			Tally (e.g., activities, exposures of advertisements, advertising products, etc.).
Qualified staff member(s) assigned to public relations					X				Inspection.
Amount of staff time spent on public relations						X			Tally.
3.10 RELATIONS WITH COMMUNITY AGENCIES									
Number of formal groups served per annum						X			Tally. Would include non-school groups, such as service and cultural organizations, city hall, etc. Included in *OMC*.

Table 1. Continued

	PLDS	OMPL OMC	FSCS	ALD	E+	E	D	D+	Notes
3.10 (continued) Number of non-service interactions with other agencies' service points						x			Tally (e.g., service on committees, speeches, etc.).
3.11 COMMUNITY ANALYSIS Utilization of community studies in library decisions					x			x	Inspection. Easy to determine existence; performing community study is not easy.

<table>
<tr><td colspan="10" align="center">Dimension 4: Access to Materials</td></tr>
</table>

	PLDS	OMPL OMC	FSCS	ALD	E+	E	D	D+	Notes
4.1 COOPERATION WITH OTHER LIBRARIES Cooperative activities with other libraries, including state library agency					x				Inspection.
Membership in a formal library cooperative					x				Inspection.
4.2 SPEED OF SERVICE Turnaround hours for service requests							x		Tally.
Turnaround days for reserves, interlibrary and intrasystem borrowings	x					x			Tally. In *OMPL:* "Document delivery"; and in Hatry and others 1992, 58: "Measure 8: Percentage of requests available within 7, 14, and 30 days."
User satisfaction with turnaround time							x		Survey. See Hatry and others 1992, 58: "Measure 9: Percentage of persons using library who rate speed of service (e.g., book retrieval and check-out) as satisfactory."
4.3 INFORMATION ABOUT OTHER COLLECTIONS Subscriptions to state-wide, regional, or national holdings databases, manual or electronic						x			Inspection of the extent of information about other collections.
4.4 INTERLIBRARY LOAN Number of interlibrary (i.e., intersystem) borrowings per annum	x		x		x				Tally.
Interlibrary borrowings fill rate	x	x				x			Tally. In *OMPL,* see "document delivery."

Table 1. Continued

	PLDS	OMPL OMC	FSCS	ALD	E+	E	D	D+	Notes
4.5 MATERIALS AVAILABILITY									
Fill rates by types of search (subject, author, title, browsing, homework)	x	x				x			Survey. In *OMPL* and *OMC*.
Probability of materials ownership							x		Complex tally of titles held as a % of standard lists, such as *BPR*, *BIP*, *Public Library Catalog*. See DeProspo, Altman, and Beasley 1973.
Availability of materials owned							x		Complex tally of materials on the shelf as a % of materials owned. See DeProspo, Altman, and Beasley 1973.
Overall user success rate							x		Survey. See Van House, Weil, and McClure 1990.
4.6 EXTENT SERVICES ARE FREE									
Variety of services, materials, and facilities available free of charge					x				Inspection (e.g., videos, reserves, online and CD searching, photoreproduction, computer uses, meeting room use).

<table>
<tr><td colspan="10" align="center">Dimension 5: Physical Facilities</td></tr>
</table>

	PLDS	OMPL OMC	FSCS	ALD	E+	E	D	D+	Notes
5.1 CONVENIENCE OF BUILDING LOCATION									
Convenience of site					x		x		Easier by inspection. Hard by survey. See Hatry and others 1992, 59: "Measure 15: Percentage of users who rate convenience as satisfactory" and "Measure 16: Percentage of non-user households who give poor physical accessability as a reason for non-use."
5.2 BUILDING EASY TO IDENTIFY									
Building clearly identifiable from the street					x				Inspection. See Hatry and others 1992, 76: "Measure 15," above.
5.3 PARKING									
Number of parking spaces					x		x		Tally of total spaces (e.g., in dedicated lot or within *x* blocks). Or survey. See Hatry and others 1992, 64: "Ease in parking."
Availability of parking spaces							x		Tally of % of spaces open.
5.4 BUILDING SUITABILITY									
Square footage per capita				x					Available data.
Seating capacity per capita				x					Tally.

Table 1. Continued

	PLDS	OMPL OMC	FSCS	ALD	E+	E	D	D+	Notes
5.4 (continued)									
Suitability of furniture and equipment							x		Survey. See Hatry and others 1992, 59: "Measure 13: Percentage of persons using library who rate the comfort, crowdedness, noise, cleanliness, and temperature/ventilation as satisfactory" and "Measure 14: Percentage of non-user households who cite lack of comfort, crowdedness, noise, cleanliness, and temperature/ventilation as reasons for non-use." See also Willett 1992, after Harms' various environmental rating scales.
Intensity of use of facilities						x			Tally. See Van House and others 1987; DeProspo, Altman, and Beasley 1973.
5.5 BUILDING APPEAL									
Appeal of library interior					x	x			Easier by personal inspection.
. . . and of library exterior					x	x			Easy by expert inspection.

Dimension 6: Boundary Spanning

	PLDS	OMPL OMC	FSCS	ALD	E+	E	D	D+	Notes
6.1 POLITICAL AND FISCAL VIABILITY OF THE LIBRARY (Indicator #62)									
Ratio of actual revenue to potential library revenue							x		Available data, using estimate of potential revenue from tax base.
Size of budget compared to similar libraries	x		x			x			Inspection of comparative data, such as *PLDS* and *FSCS*.
Stability of funding						x			Available data with additional calculation (e.g., % increase/decrease of budget compared to a base year; or increase/decrease of library budget compared to other services).
Political success of the library					x				Inspection.
6.2 BOARD ACTIVENESS									
Activeness of library board					x				Easier by inspection. Easy by tally of board attendance at meetings, education events, conferences, etc.
Orientation of new board members					x				Inspection.
Written bylaws for board, reviewed regularly					x				Inspection.

Table 1. Continued

	PLDS	OMPL OMC	FSCS	ALD	E+	E	D	D+	Notes
6.3 Voluntary Contributions (Gifts, Money, Time)									
Dollar value of gifts of money, materials, equipment						x			Tally.
Hours of volunteer time per annum						x			Tally.
Dollars raised through effort of volunteers						x			Tally.
Activeness of Friends or other volunteers in the library's political arena					x				Inspection.
6.4 Library Products (Booklists, Guides, etc.)									
Number of library productions, publications, and recordings distributed per annum per capita					x				Tally.
6.5 Energy Efficiency of Building									
Energy efficiency							x		Expert inspection.
Participation in a recycling program					x				Inspection.
6.6 Continuing Education for Staff									
Number of hours of continuing education attended + staff member						x			Tally.
Number of continuing education events attended per staff member						x			Tally.
Percentage of staff participating in continuing education						x			Tally.
6.7 Planning and Evaluation									
Long-range, written plan					x				Inspection.
Long-term assessment of space needs					x				Inspection.
Annual review and adjustment of plan					x				Inspection.
Evaluation of library activities and programs					x				Inspection.
6.8 Public Involvement in Library Decisions									
Defined mechanism for community input to design and development of services and facilities					x				Inspection.
Complaints procedure for users						x			Inspection.
Public access to board meetings and board documents						x			Inspection.

Table 1. Continued

	PLDS	OMPL OMC	FSCS	ALD	E+	E	D	D+	Notes
Dimension 7: Service Offerings									
7.1 RANGE OF MATERIALS									
Variety of formats of materials						x			Inspection (e.g., computer software, book, journal, slide, audio disc, audio cassette, video cassette, optical disc, etc.).
Number of items in each format			x			x			Available data or tally.
Breadth of subjects in library's collections						x			Inspection.
Depth of holdings in library's collections							x		Inspection.
7.2 RANGE OF SERVICES									
Number of services offered					x				Inspection. See appendix B, "Checklist of Library Services."
Extent to which library offers all of its services when open					x				Inspection.
Innovative program of services					x				Inspection.
7.3 CONVENIENCE OF HOURS									
Number of hours open per week		x			x				Tally. In *FSCS:* "Sum of hours of all outlets" ("duplicated hours").
Range of hours open		x			x				Tally. In *FSCS:* "Hours during which a user can find service at one outlet or another" ("unduplicated hours."
Convenience to users of hours open							x		Survey. See Hatry and others 1992, 59: "Measure 18: Percentage of user households rating hours of opening as satisfactory" and "Measure 19: Percentage of non-user households who give poor hours as a reason for non-use."
Users, by hour							x		Tally. Convenience as reflected in the volume of activity in the various hour blocks.
7.4 MATERIALS QUALITY									
Collection quality							x		Can be addressed through the tallies and surveys of "turnover rate" (dimension 1), "materials availability" (dimension 4), and "currency of collection" (dimension 7). See also Hatry and others 1992, 58: "Measure 7b: Percentage of users who rate materials as satisfactory" and "Measure 7c: Percentage of non-users who cite poor materials as a reason for non-use." Can also be addressed through the

Table 1. Continued

	PLDS	OMPL OMC	FSCS	ALD	E+	E	D	D+	Notes
7.4 (continued)									conspectus approach (systematic inspection), as presented in Bryant 1989. See Lancaster 1988, 17–32, where alternative approaches to the complex issue of evaluating collections are discussed.
7.5 NEWNESS OF MATERIALS									
Median publication date							x		Tally.
New volumes per annum					x				Available data.
. . . and per capita					x				Available data.
Titles added as a % of total titles, per annum					x				Tally.
Speed of acquisitions						x			Tally (i.e., median lapsed time between release date of a publication and its appearance on the shelves).

Dimension 8: Service to Special Groups

	PLDS	OMPL OMC	FSCS	ALD	E+	E	D	D+	Notes
8.1 HANDICAPPED ACCESS									
Handicapped accessibility						x	x		Inspection, or expert inspection. See King Research Ltd. 1990, 19: ". . . existence of facilities, such as wheelchair ramps and parking spaces, or by rating degree of accessibility using scales (1 to 5)"; and *Code of Federal Regulations* 1990, 576–91, for federal regulations regarding architectural barriers for the handicapped.
8.2 SPECIAL GROUP SERVICES									
Services to populations with special needs						x	x		Inspection, or expert inspection (e.g., the homebound and institutionalized, ethnic minorities, the aged, underemployed, business and labor, local government).

Conclusion

This chapter has presented AMPLE in two versions: the complete AMPLE, derived from the responses of more than 2,500 people representing seven major public library constituencies, and the short AMPLE, consisting of the most highly ranked indicators. AMPLE is a set of dimensions, indicators, and suggested measures that can be used to identify the categories within which a library will want to assess itself, to determine the completeness of the library's own system of assessment, and to develop or refine its assessment. In this chapter, we have presented some advice on using AMPLE to develop a set of measures for your library.

The next chapter looks more closely at a critical issue in the assessment of public libraries as public sector organizations: identifying and addressing the priorities of the library's many and varied constituencies.

References

American Library Directory, 1991–1992. 1991. New York: R. R. Bowker.

Berelson, Bernard. 1949. *The Library's Public.* New York: Columbia University Press.

Bryant, Bonita. 1989. *Guide for Written Collection Policy Statements.* Chicago: American Library Association.

Code of Federal Regulations 36, Chap. XI (July 1, 1990). Washington, D.C.: Office of the Federal Register, National Archives and Records Administration.

Damanpour, Fariborz, and Thomas Childers. 1985. "The Adoption of Innovations in Public Libraries." *Library and Information Science Research* 7 (July–September): 231–46.

D'Elia, George, and Sandra Walsh. 1983. "User Satisfaction with Library Service—A Measure of Public Library Performance?" *Library Quarterly* 53 (April): 109–33.

DeProspo, Ernest R., Ellen Altman, and Kenneth E. Beasley. 1973. *Performance Measures for Public Libraries.* Chicago: American Library Association.

Hatry, Harry P., Louis H. Blair, Donald M. Fisk, John M. Greiner, John R. Hall, Jr., and Philip S. Schaenman. 1992. *How Effective Are Your Community Services? Procedures for Measuring Their Quality,* 2nd ed. Washington, D.C.: Urban Institute and the International City/County Management Association.

Kaske, Neal, Annabel Stephens, and Philip Turner. 1986. "Alabama's Public Libraries as Seen by Patrons, Administrators, and Trustees." Tuscaloosa: University of Alabama (typescript).

King Research, Ltd. 1990. *Keys to Success: Performance Indicators for Public Libraries.* London: Office of Arts and Libraries.

Lancaster, F. W. 1988. *If You Want to Evaluate Your Library . . . .* Champaign: University of Illinois.

Public Library Data Service Statistical Report '90. Annual. Chicago: Public Library Association.

Task Force on Federal-State Cooperative System for Public Library Data. 1989. *An Action Plan for a Federal-State Cooperative System for Public Library Data.* Washington, D.C.: U.S. National Commission on Libraries and Information Science; National Center for Education Statistics.

Van House, Nancy A., and Thomas Childers. 1993. *The Public Library Effectiveness Study: The Complete Report.* Chicago: American Library Association.

Van House, Nancy A., Mary Jo Lynch, Charles R. McClure, Douglas L. Zweizig, and Eleanor Jo Rodger. 1987. *Output Measures for Public Libraries,* 2nd ed. Chicago: American Library Association.

Van House, Nancy A., Beth T. Weil, and Charles R. McClure. 1990. *Measuring Academic Library Performance: A Practical Approach.* Chicago: American Library Association.

Walter, Virginia. 1992. *Output Measures for Public Library Service to Children.* Chicago: American Library Association.

Willett, Holly G. 1992. "Designing an Evaluation Instrument: The Environment Rating Scale in Process." *Journal of Youth Services in Libraries* 49, no. 2 (Winter): 165–73.

Applying AMPLE

7

On the use of AMPLE, with lessons from writers and practicing librarians about how to communicate with stakeholders, especially the critical external ones.

Talking to Stakeholders, Generally

Indicators and measures of effectiveness are useful internally and externally. Internally, they provide information that can be the basis for decisions about controlling and planning library operations (such as circulation processes, acquisitions policy, or staff scheduling). Externally, indicators and measures of effectiveness can be a basis for setting the library's direction and mix of service offerings, vis-à-vis its community; for taking action in the social, economic, and political context; and for communicating with the individuals and groups who influence library-related decisions.

From here on, the book concentrates on external decisions and on the "contextual" stakeholders—the externals, who influence the library's future from outside, and the boundary-spanners, whose influence is partially inside, partially outside the library.

We have said throughout this book that the task of the library manager is both to assess library performance and to present it to others. For a library to get the resources that it needs, performing well is not sufficient. People who have power over library decisions, if they are not themselves clients of the library, cannot directly assess organizational performance. And even those who are clients can generally assess only a small part of it. The library has to find a way to communicate its effectiveness to the

political decision-makers in a way that is useful for both the library and the decision-makers.

> *Managers must stay well attuned to the personal and political dynamics of the groups with whom they deal. But good decisions cannot be made without good information.* (Chase and Reveal 1983, 134)

The choice of indicators to use in evaluating an organization is, according to MacRae (1985, 293), "a political question and not simply a scientific one." He claims that among the political considerations that contribute to the choice are the:

- greater needs of the society or community that must be attended to (such as reducing illiteracy, empowering the powerless, sharing cultures, or strengthening the economy);
- more particular information needs of the stakeholders in arriving at decisions (what kind of information they want, or will use—at what depth and breadth, and in which formats); and
- costs of generating—collecting, tabulating, analyzing, preparing, publishing, etc.—the information.

If assessment is intended to produce information for political decision-making, the library has to determine who its political audiences are and what they most want to know. What the audiences want to know may well be different from what the library thinks they need to know.

Up to this point, we have dealt with the model as a whole, looking at the library's whole program of assessment. This chapter considers how to use AMPLE in more targeted communication with individual stakeholder groups. First we discuss how one talks with stakeholders about the effectiveness of a public sector organization; then we address the public library's specific stakeholders and what they are likely to want to know.

In the political arena, those deciding whether to support an organization look at three things (Heymann 1987, 1):

1. what the organization does that affects their interests;
2. what its activities and interests say about what is important to the organization and whose concerns or views are to be given weight; and
3. what alliances with powerful organizations and individuals its words and actions seem intended to build.

Stakeholders' interests certainly vary over space and time. Part of building an assessment program and creating a communication strategy is to identify the agendas of your stakeholders. This is an essential part of talking to them, of representing the library to them.

> You are what you measure.

The information that the library uses to describe itself also tells the observer what and who the library thinks is important, what its goals are, what it has been able to achieve and, by implication, what it can accomplish in the future. If the library monitors its service to children, for example, it is saying that children are important—that the library is concerned enough about its services to children to assess them separately, as well as that it can be of use to children. Similarly, materials and services to ethnic and language minorities demonstrate the library's interest in contributing to these communities. But the library must also demonstrate that the library is providing services used by the target groups—that is, that the library is successful.

> *Knowledge should be interesting, understandable, and relevant to your interests.*
> (John Scully, quoted in Wurman 1989, 185)

Representing an organization's effectiveness is equivalent to arguing for what it needs: money, attention, appreciation, patronage, security, a change in the environment, and so on. Chief among the arguments (Pfeffer and Salancik 1978, 193–97) is that the organization is *legitimate*—that its goals are valid. Legitimacy may need to be argued strenuously in the case of some organizations. Welfare organizations of all types are continually pressed to evidence their legitimacy, for example. Other organizations, such as police, are rarely questioned on their legitimacy.

The public library may fall somewhere in between. It is probably widely accepted among the various stakeholders that the public library has a valid position in the community; but the exact nature of that position and the amount of community resource required to maintain it there are unclear. It is up to library management, in communicating to the external stakeholders, to direct the representations of library effectiveness so as to establish the legitimacy of the library in the stakeholders' minds—to argue for the worthiness of the library's program of activities.

Since establishing legitimacy "generally implies that an organization reviews its past actions and outputs in the context of current societal values and interests" (Pfeffer and Salancik 1978, 195), it is critical for the library to communicate in terms that relate to the *current* social scenery, whatever that may be.

Information can also be used to control to some extent the expectations that others have of the organization (Pfeffer and Salancik 1978). By focusing the information presented, library management can, to some degree, set the criteria of goodness and badness ("The library circulated 2.3 titles per capita, and that needs improvement; we contacted 47 percent of school-aged children this year, and that is good.").

The outside world—the public, elected officials, budget officers, and so on—comes to many public institutions and, specifically, libraries, with low or undeveloped expectations. They frequently consider, when the per capita cost of the service is relatively low and the perceived per capita benefit is low (Wilson 1989) or uncertain, that there is little at stake and that virtually any benefit received is valuable. Generally, the public has little idea of the full program of library services and the parameters within which a library can be effective. Does a library give answers to users' questions? Which media should a library offer? How many users per capita should there be? What is an acceptable turnover rate for a book? How much should a library cost? How many professional staff should there be? Moreover, the difficulty of observing the activities of a service organization—with fleeting interpersonal transactions, often observable only to its participants—places the organization itself in the primary position for reporting on its activities.

In speaking to its political audience, the library has to consider not just the content, but the manner of the presentation:

New information must fit into what we already know. People naturally seek to make a connection between new data and their existing map of the world and prior experience (Wurman 1989). The task of the manager, then, is to use that prior knowledge to help people to understand the library appropriately because they will indeed use their prior knowledge, whether appropriately or not. Unfortunately, most of its audience believes that they know more about the

> *You only learn something relative to something you understand.* (Wurman 1989, 168)

library than they do and may be resistant to changing their mental image. Budget officers, for example, may be so used to circulation as a measure of library goodness, finding it easy to calculate and understand, facilitating instant cross-library and cross-branch comparisons, that it may be difficult to get them to listen to another, especially a more complex, measure, such as item-use-day or even total annual uses.

Information must be presented in terms that the audience will understand. Generally, one must understand their point of view and prior knowledge. This means using their language, drawing parallels with other things that they already know and care about (services, events, and so on), presenting information in easily understood and familiar ways. "Materials turnover" doesn't mean much to outsiders; "average use per item" is more understandable; and "return on materials investment" is even more so.

Information must be put in context. A circulation per capita of 7.5 per annum means little to the external stakeholders. The highest circulation per capita in the region, however, or a circulation per capita 20 percent higher than a rival county—these get attention. One hundred thousand library users per month may impress those insiders who know that last year it was only 50,000 per month; for those who don't, a more impressive statement is, "More people used the library than attended sporting events in this sports-proud city." Every city councilmember knows what a full football stadium looks like. The comparisons make the data intelligible.

Another example comes from Sam Clay,

director of the Fairfax County Public Library, through a personal communication: "I lose in books each year the cost equivalent of three fire trucks." After that revelation, his funding authorities' challenges to the need for a new security system ceased. Interestingly, this is a story than can be built only on statistics. You

> *Numbers become meaningful only when they can be related to concepts that can be viscerally grasped.* (Wurman 1989, 178)

have to have the data in order to make the comparisons. But it nicely illustrates the lessons of "meet them on their own terms" and "tell them a story," for it translates numbers (dollars, volumes, and so on) into terms that have immediate associative—almost visual—power, vis-à-vis one of the funder's prominent headaches, the notorious cost of replacing fire trucks.

> *You have to build off things you understand. Comparisons enable recognition.* (Wurman 1989, 178)

Local government is very concerned with "spatial data—comparing conditions in local neighborhoods" (MacRae 1985, 305) for at least two reasons: the comparisons help make sense of the data (if this branch has the lowest use per capita of any in town, that's probably not good), and an enduring public concern is equity of services across neighborhoods and socioeconomic groups. Therefore, most library managers want data that compare neighborhood with neighborhood. Many of the measures in AMPLE can be subdivided for localities within a city. This is especially true in larger urban settings, where good assessment can show a complex picture of pluralistic, heterogeneous communities and can draw a picture of service that compares locality to locality. Indicators related to service offered and service used—such as the numbers of materials owned, visits to the library, reference volume—are likely to vary within a system of library outlets.

Convey the message vividly and succinctly. Graphics can convey complex information memorably and quickly. The proliferation of computers with graphics capabilities has made this easy; but it has also led to an epidemic of bad graphics. Several sources discuss the use of graphics for quantitative data. We refer you particularly to the inspiring *Envisioning Information* (Tufte 1990).

This is not intended to be a tutorial in creating graphics, but some considerations for creating good graphics are worth noting:

- A graphic should be able to stand on its own. It shouldn't require text to explain it. People sitting in an audience looking at overheads or readers thumbing through a report may not listen to or read your explanation; and a graphic often gets photocopied and separated from its text. Is your graphic presented and labelled clearly enough to speak for itself?

- Don't try to do too much with one graphic. Decide what you most want to convey and do it. Are you trying to show changes over time, or differences across branches? Changes in absolute magnitude, or in relative size?

- Test out your graphics. Show them to someone uninformed about the subject. Ask that person to paraphrase the graphics; ask what questions the graphics leave unanswered.

In learning to do graphics, pay attention to what you see—in the newspaper, in other people's reports, wherever—and notice which ones work well, and why.

Some examples of very compelling displays of data were found a few years ago in *Egg* magazine in a report on the quality of life at selected recreational sites in Los Angeles (McAuley 1990). Figure 17 shows the data on the "Chance of Stepping in Something Gross."

The report and its data displays were designed to provoke, outrage, and amuse at least as much as to inform. It is doubtful that any

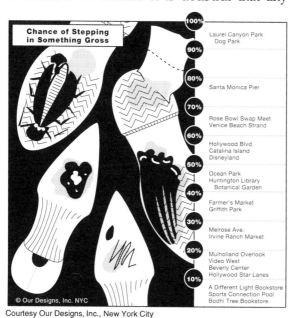

Courtesy Our Designs, Inc., New York City

Figure 17. Chance of Stepping in Something Gross

hard data were collected in this case. But the lesson is that the displays easily capture the reader's attention and make a simple point, with impact. The lesson is that *presentation* can be as important as the data in communicating a message of effectiveness. Displays of library data could employ *Egg*-type techniques, invoking the provocative, outrageous, and amusing elements, judiciously. Messages with social, economic, political, and performance meaning can be communicated vividly and succinctly to the stakeholders—messages such as the impact of materials expenditures on circulation; or hours open on visits to the library.

The Colorado State Library, for years, has supported a Library Research Service. It regularly investigates questions related to the effectiveness of Colorado's libraries and reports them to libraries and library stakeholders. All of the reports are easily read and understood by people without training in research or conversant in data displays.

One of the services, Peer Data for Colorado Academic Libraries, generates and displays comparative data on selected library measures. The bar chart for materials expenditures is shown in figure 18. The Colorado example relies on pre-existing computer software and, unlike the *Egg* display, uses cut-and-paste rather than original artwork. The value of this kind of presentation is that it offers comparative data to external stakeholders who may need to be educated in the standards of goodness for the various aspects of libraries. This example can easily be translated for public library applications, and the Public Library Data Service and FSCS provide the raw material for doing so.

Another example from Colorado, directly related to public libraries, concerns the salaries of public library directors (Colorado State Library and Adult Education Office 1991) (figure 19). It would be easy to mark the salary of the local director on this histogram, for comparative purposes.

Stories vs. Data

Storytelling is another way of putting information in context and giving you memory.   (Wurman 1989, 237)

Data, even graphically presented, are not the only, or even always the best, way to convey information. People remember vivid stories better than abstract arguments. They remember

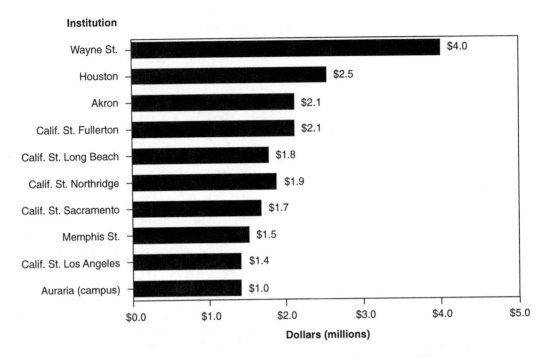

Figure 18. Materials Expenditures for Auraria Library and Selected Peer Libraries, 1990

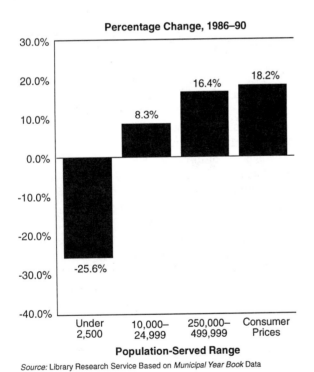

Source: Library Research Service Based on *Municipal Year Book* Data

Figure 19. Average Salary Increases for Western Public Library Directors in Selected Population Ranges, 1986–90

best of all that which happens to themselves; then the stories that they hear firsthand from participants; and finally good stories that they hear from other sources. In our interviews,

many local officials illustrated their points with stories told to them by their constituents. Oral traditions have relied on myths and parables to convey principles for living—for good reason.

We all know the impact of stories of personal achievement and failure:

> a welfare mother who became independent after participating in the library's graduate equivalency diploma program;
>
> the author who was inspired by library materials to write the great American novel;
>
> the underachiever who was turned around by the caring librarian; and
>
> the student who could not do an assignment because the materials weren't there.

There are also examples in the public library field of anecdotes and data being merged. One of the best of recent years is found in the popular report of the five-year plan of the Free Library of Philadelphia (1991). The report consists of the library's role statements interleaved with its goals and objectives, current data on users, and quotations and photographs of library users. A composite illustration of several pages is shown in Figure 20. Note that the "anecdote" is told in the photograph and quotation of the user, which relates directly to the library's role—"Answer Place"—which, in turn, relates directly to the data presented.

ROLE 2: THE ANSWER PLACE

People expect to find something about everything at the library. Whether it's a question related to a business plan, a vacation idea, a homework assignment, or a new career, people want answers.

ERIC W. JOHNSON

"I call the reference department one or two hundred times a year! I think the librarians are very close to saints. They'll look through several books in detail in order to answer a question. I feel as if I have the world at my ear."

GOAL 1:   MORE ACCURATE, UP-TO-DATE
          REFERENCE INFORMATION

'94   • Create easier access to library holdings with a
         better on-line computer catalog.

       • Update community information collections and
         agency files annually.

GOAL 2:   FASTER REFERENCE INFORMATION

'93   • Determine feasibility of a central library periodical
         center.

       • Increase available shelf space at central library.

       • Upgrade the telephone system; include portable
         phones and automatic answering machines

'94   • Provide dial-in access to the on-line catalog on
         weekends and evenings.

'95   • Establish a network for information delivery
         between all branches for same-day delivery of
         documents.

       • Create a telephone reference service for hours
         the library is not open.

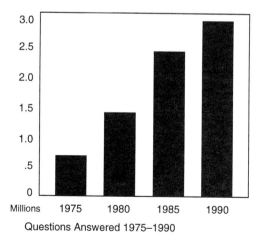

Questions Answered 1975–1990

Figure 20. Role 2: The Answer Place

Talking to the Particular Stakeholders

Moving from general issues in talking with stakeholders, the rest of this chapter considers the *public library's* various stakeholder groups, what they most want to know about the library, and how to use AMPLE to design a system of assessing and communicating library goodness in a multifaceted political environment.

AMPLE works as a checklist for highlighting the indicators and, subordinately, measures that are preferred by the library's stakeholders *in general*, and by *particular stakeholders* or *stakeholder types* whom you have identified as key actors in your library's future. Obviously, this is part of building a program of assessment, and it moves us toward the *communication* aspect of representing the library.

In identifying stakeholders, you should keep in mind that *individuals* may hold several different stakes in the organization. This is certainly true with regard to libraries. A possible explanation for the similarity of indicator rankings among the seven stakeholder groups of the Public Library Effectiveness Study is that they *all* played the role of library user at some point in their lives. Their responses may have been somewhat homogenized and the differences, role to role (stake to stake), obscured. It is conceivable that the same person would occupy the role of local official and library user; or of community leader and trustee; or of user and friend of the library.

Further, Pfeffer and Salancik (1978, 30–31) assert that it is *sets of behaviors*, rather than individuals, that should provide the focus for identifying the organization's external forces. A gross way of enumerating behaviors is to identify the variety of *key roles* played in the library's environment (as well as internally)—identifying stakeholder groups for your library on the basis of the various stakeholding roles being played. Only then would one identify the *persons* to communicate with regarding the library.

Stakeholders are generally classified as internal (members of the organization) or external. However, this classification is a continuum, not a dichotomy, as people vary in the extent to which they belong to the organization. Mills (1986), for example, says that users of service organizations, especially those where self-service or coproduction is significant (see chapter 4), are partial members of the organization.

Stakeholders, via the Public Library Effectiveness Study

The Public Library Effectiveness Study surveyed members of seven key public library constituent groups and asked what indicators they would find useful in evaluating or describing the library. (Chapter 5 describes the groups in detail and presents the study method.) We found slight differences in survey responses across groups. In the in-depth interviews with selected respondents, and in subsequent discussions with library leaders, we heard much greater differences across constituent groups, leading us to

believe that our survey instrument was not sensitive or comprehensive enough to fully reflect the differences among groups. The discussion in this chapter about constituent group desires and preferences, therefore, is based on the survey responses, the interviews, other discussions with public library leaders, and the writings of other analysts concerned with decision-making and organizational effectiveness in the public sector.

Figure 21 summarizes the responses of the seven constituent groups surveyed. One of the first things that jumps off the matrix is that several indicators are held as "very important" by all stakeholder groups:

Staff Quality
Efficiency of Library Operations
Staff Helpfulness
Community Awareness of Offerings
Services Suited to the Community
Materials Availability
Convenience of Building Location
Range of Materials
Range of Services
Convenience of Hours
Materials Quality

Yet there are points of disagreement. In what follows, we will discuss expected and observed differences among the stakeholder groups, possible reasons for these differences, and how to use this information in talking to constituent groups. Later in this chapter, we will discuss methods of presenting the AMPLE data.

External Stakeholders

Pfeffer and Salancik (1978) assert that the external ("contextual") forces are critical in determining the fate of an organization because they control the resources without which there would be no organization. The entire range of external stakeholders is often difficult to identify. For a complex public institution, such as a library, the individuals and groups who have actual or potential power over decisions about the library can be varied and hidden. The resources that they control are of two basic kinds: the purse strings, and the attention of those appointed and elected officials who control the purse strings.

It seems to us—and there is a lot of literature in support—that many public libraries have not been good at the care and feeding of the external stakeholders in the past and long to know how to talk to them, persuade them, sell them on the library program. That is, public libraries have

	CL	LO	FR	TR	US	LM	LS
Dimension 1: Traditional Counts							
Uses and Users	†	†	†	*	‡	*	*
Visits to Library	†	*	†	*	‡	*	*
Circulation	†	*	†	*	‡	*	*
Reference Volume	‡	‡	‡	‡	‡	†	‡
Variety of Users	‡	‡	‡	‡	‡	‡	‡
Materials Turnover	‡	‡	‡	‡	‡	‡	‡
Materials Expenditure	‡	†	†	†	†	*	*
Total Expenditures	†	†	‡	†	‡	†	†
Program Attendance	†	†	‡	‡	‡	‡	‡
In-Library Use	‡	‡	‡	‡	‡	‡	‡
Materials Owned	†	†	†	†	†	†	*
Staff Size	‡	‡	‡	‡	‡	†	†
Reference Fill Rate	†	‡	‡	‡	†	*	†
Staff Expenditures	‡	‡	‡	†	‡	‡	‡
Equipment Usage	‡	‡	‡	‡	‡	‡	‡
Use of Library Compared to Other Service Events	‡	‡	‡	‡	‡	‡	‡
Dimension 2: Internal Processes							
Managerial Competence	*	*	*	*	†	†	*
Staff Morale	†	†	*	*	*	*	*
Staff Quality	*	*	*	*	*	*	*
Staff Helpfulness	*	*	*	*	*	*	*
Support of Intellectual Freedom	†	‡	*	†	*	†	†
Efficiency of Library Operations	*	*	*	*	*	*	*
Written Policies	‡	‡	‡	†	‡	†	†
Goal Achievement	†	†	†	*	†	†	†
Safety of Users	‡	‡	†	‡	†	‡	‡
Dimension 3: Community Fit							
Community Awareness of Offerings	*	*	*	*	*	*	*
Users' Evaluation	*	*	†	*	†	*	*
Contribution to Community Well-Being	*	*	*	*	†	†	*
Services Suited to the Community	*	*	*	*	*	*	*
Public Opinion	*	*	*	*	†	*	*
Flexibility of Library Management	*	†	†	*	†	†	†
Staff Suited to Community	†	†	†	†	†	†	†
Public Relations	‡	‡	†	†	‡	‡	†

* = Very important indicator (i.e., within the top 20 for that stakeholder group)
† = Important indicator (i.e., between 21 and 40 for that stakeholder group)
‡ = Not very important indicator (i.e., between 41 and 61 for that stakeholder group)
§ = Rating data were not collected on this indicator.

Figure 21. Stakeholders' Preferences for Indicators

(continued)

	CL	LO	FR	TR	US	LM	LS
Dimension 3: (continued)							
Staff Contact with Users	†	‡	†	†	†	†	†
Relations with Community Agencies	†	‡	‡	‡	‡	‡	‡
Community Analysis	‡	‡	‡	‡	‡	‡	‡
Dimension 4: Access to Materials							
Information about Other Collections	‡	‡	†	‡	†	‡	‡
Inter-Library Loans	‡	‡	‡	‡	†	‡	‡
Cooperation with Other Libraries	†	†	†	†	*	‡	†
Speed of Service	*	*	*	†	*	*	†
Materials Availability	*	*	*	*	*	*	*
Extent Services Are Free	*	*	*	†	*	†	†
Dimension 5: Physical Facilities							
Convenience of Building Location	*	*	*	*	*	*	*
Building Easy to Identify	†	†	*	†	†	*	†
Parking	*	†	†	†	*	†	‡
Building Suitability	†	†	†	†	*	†	†
Building Appeal	†	†	†	‡	†	‡	‡
Dimension 6: Boundary Spanning							
Political and Fiscal Viability of the Library	§	§	§	§	§	§	§
Board Activeness	‡	‡	‡	‡	‡	‡	‡
Voluntary Contributions	‡	‡	‡	‡	‡	‡	‡
Library Products	‡	†	‡	‡	†	‡	‡
Energy Efficiency of Building	‡	‡	‡	‡	‡	‡	‡
Continuing Education for Staff	‡	‡	‡	‡	†	‡	‡
Planning and Evaluation	†	†	†	†	†	†	†
Public Involvement in Library Decisions	‡	‡	‡	‡	‡	‡	‡
Dimension 7: Service Offerings							
Range of Materials	*	*	*	*	*	*	*
Range of Services	*	*	*	*	*	*	*
Convenience of Hours	*	*	*	*	*	*	*
Materials Quality	*	*	*	*	*	*	*
Newness of Materials	*	†	†	†	*	†	†
Dimension 8: Service to Special Groups							
Handicapped Access	*	*	*	†	*	†	†
Special Group Services	†	*	*	†	*	†	†

* = Very important indicator (i.e., within the top 20 for that stakeholder group)
† = Important indicator (i.e., between 21 and 40 for that stakeholder group)
‡ = Not very important indicator (i.e., between 41 and 61 for that stakeholder group)
§ = Rating data were not collected on this indicator.

Figure 21. (continued)

been representing themselves better to the internal than to the external interests. Thus, this book spends a large amount of time on communicating with the contextual stakeholders.

The external constituencies of the public library identified in the Public Library Effectiveness Study and their particular interests are as follows.

Elected officials. According to Heymann (1987; 126–27), legislators have five major categories of concern:

1. the merits of the proposal: both what they think is good for their jurisdiction and what they believe the contituents with whom they identify are entitled to on this occasion;
2. what their votes will mean in terms of maintaining electoral support;
3. how their positions and actions will affect their influence on other matters;
4. what is required for the continued health of the legislative process as a whole; and
5. demands of loyalty and friendship.

A group of public library leaders (Van House and Childers 1991, 275) identified the major current social and political concerns which affect officials' (and the public's) assessment of the public library—the pressing issues in their jurisdictions and for their constituents—which relate to the public library as:

• economic development, including attracting and nurturing business, bolstering job opportunities and job preparedness, and facilitating the job search;
• education of the citizenry, largely as a supplement to a failing public education system;
• the appeal of service agencies to diverse audiences, with special attention to the non-English speaking, the illiterate, and the disadvantaged; and
• the quality of management of the public enterprise, which includes demonstrating productivity, being a good team player, demonstrating political *savoir faire,* and educating them about what the library can do and the criteria by which it is to be judged. The last point directly led these two authors to conceive and write this book.

We would expect elected officials to be most concerned with library outputs and outcomes (impact on the community), and with which parts of the community are being served. In our interviews, we also found that they were concerned with the broader public sector issues that concern the citizenry, including waste, equity of services, and, in general, managerial competence as a determinant of efficiency in the use of public resources. Since elected officials depend on the voting public for their continued electoral success, their concerns have to echo those of their constituents.

Elected officials are also concerned about how their vote on library matters fits into the larger political decision-making structure. For example, a city councilmember in a city with district elections told us that, in matters concerning a branch library in another district, he would defer to the wishes of the councilmember for that district, and would expect her to do the same on issues affecting his district.

The Public Library Effectiveness Study results generally confirm these expectations (see figure 21): local officials were most concerned with the indicators that fell under commuity fit, Internal Processes, Service Offerings, and Services to Special Groups. (Note that the Public Library Effectiveness Study did not distinguish between elected and appointed local officials.)

Appointed officials. Appointed officials want to succeed in their jobs and to look good to the elected officials and the public (who influence elected officials) in order to earn the support they need to do their jobs. A good library director helps his or her superiors avoid headaches and create success (Chase and Reveal 1983). When the library gets attention, the attention should be positive and reflect well on the library and local government (Van House and Childers 1991).

In looking at the library, we would expect appointed officials to share the elected officials' concerns for results and for the distributional impact of services. In addition, they would be more concerned about internal organizational processes. A city manager told us that he didn't know what a good library should do, but as a manager he knew a good manager when he saw one and could trust him or her to run a good library. The key indicator of effectiveness for this city official is Managerial Competence—which can be obliquely suggested in many ways (economy of operation; good budget; stable staff; high use by the public; and so on), but is very hard to measure directly.

The general public. The public consists of consumers or potential consumers of public services; it also includes the taxpayers who support them. They are concerned about specific programs and services for themselves or client groups about whom they care, for whatever reason. For example, children, especially children at risk, are a client group about whom many in the community care.

The public also cares about power relationships and equity, what the distribution of public services says about who is important and who gets what. It is common, for example, for communities to fight for branch libraries as a symbol of their power and the attention paid to them, regardless of whether they use it.

The public also shows concern over enduring issues about the public sector's use of tax monies, including waste, corruption, and excessive government interference in people's lives (Heymann 1987), independent of the particular government unit or service under consideration.

And, finally, the public is concerned about how individual public sector decisions relate to broader social concerns, such as how library spending can help in the public education crisis or in a faltering local economy. The public is concerned that its limited tax dollars be used well, for worthwhile and cost-effective programs (see chapter 1).

The Public Library Effectiveness Study did not survey members of the general public, so we cannot confirm these expectations from our survey data. We did, however, survey two other external groups who are closely related to the general public: community leaders and library users.

Community leaders. For public libraries, community leaders include the heads of cultural, education, and media enterprises (such as museums, school districts, or newspapers), heads of influential civic organizations (such as community improvement associations or neighborhood associations), leaders of industry (such as the president of the chamber of commerce or a high-level manager of a major firm), and others who are considered to speak for the larger community. Community leaders represent, but are also often out in front of the public: they may identify problems and trends before the public as a whole does. They may see themselves as guardians of the public trust and watchdogs of public expenditures. Because community leaders are less constrained by public opinion than elected officials, they may be able to take more radical stands on some issues. Many represent or lead special interest groups.

Community leaders can be expected to care about the larger social and political agenda of their community, quality of government, and efficiency of public services, as well as issues more specific to the library, primarily services and distributional impact, secondarily internal processes. From figure 21, it appears that our community leaders were not as concerned about traditional Library Service Counts as about Community Fit and Service Offerings.

Library users. Library users are concerned about the services that they themselves use and the other characteristics of the library they value. Branch library users, for example, may know that the selection of materials is greater at the main library, but they may prefer the ambiance of the branch and its role as a neighborhood center.

Our user respondents were most concerned about materials," "service offerings," and "internal processes." The first is predictable. The second is more of a surprise until one looks at the indicators included in that dimension—many of which directly affect users, such as Staff Quality and Helpfulness. Users were the group most concerned about Physical Facilities with which, of course, they have more experience than any group other than staff. They had surprisingly little interest in the Traditional Counts with which libraries most often assess themselves.

Internal Stakeholders

As noted in chapter 4, Wilson (1989) says that external forces, such as interest groups and formal governors, influence the direction and effect of an organization. But he argues that a public organization's being is also defined by how what he calls the operators—in our case, librarians, and library technicians—and management (library directors) see their critical tasks. Indeed, the external world may mandate a broad mission for the public organization, may provide the wherewithall for success to a greater or lesser degree, and may grant or withhold the discretion to operate freely. Once such parameters are laid down, if they are sufficiently unconstraining, the public organization often has a great deal of latitude in defining its own critical focus and how it operates. The internals have major control. (Remember our city manager who said that he didn't know what a library should do.)

In fact, public libraries enjoy a wide latitude, as public organizations go, since the public tends to have a fairly simple and naive view of public libraries (often defining public library service as that which their local public library does, and no more). Some knowledgeable users have a broader conception of the library's stock-in-trade (information and information materials in many different formats). In some instances, the community has made the library a semi-independent organization (by incorporating it under a board of trustees or establishing an autonomous tax base). In such circumstances, where operating discretion is broad, Wilson (1989) says that the operating members wield tremendous influence on what the organization is or is not.

Moreover, the public library is a professional bureaucracy, as Mintzberg (1989) defines it, which is characterized by having an "operating core" that is relatively powerful. Remember the discussion in chapter 4 about the high degree of independence of professionals in a service organization characterized by indeterminant technology. The actions of individual staff members have a major impact on deciding the true operating mission of the organization.

In an environment in which staff have wide latitude and a structure where the operating core is typically strong, library professionals can be expected to play a major role in deciding the library's essential nature: whether the library serves the educational or leisure or vocational needs of the citizenry; is a utility linking citizens to all the world's information materials; offers deep or shallow collections; strives to reach the traditionally non-using public; and other things. To get a sense of just how much latitude the professionals have, consider how much variation often exists between neighboring libraries; and how much a change in top management can alter the nature of a library and its services.

Management and public services staff, however, often have somewhat different views. In many small library outlets, such as community branches, the roles of library manager and library services staff may converge in a single person. But in larger organizations, management and the public services staff may differ substantially in their roles and their views.

Public services staff. The public services staff, as boundary-spanners—that is, people at that "boundary" of the organization who interact with the external world in the person of the user—have a dual loyalty to the organization and to its clients (Hasenfeld 1983). They are often especially concerned that the library is doing what their clients need and want, and

even act as advocates for their clients. The Public Library Effectiveness Study shows their interest to be strongly focused on indicators of service quality and the resources that the library applies to service. Public service librarians, as well as library managers, place more emphasis on Traditional Counts—the measures by which libraries have customarily measured their own effectiveness — than do any other groups.

Library management. Managers have a somewhat different view than public services staff. Managers may be somewhat removed from the daily reality with which public services staff deal all the time. At the same time, managers necessarily take a larger view of the organization: While the children's services and reference staff vie for resources, the manager may have to decide whether one should be cut back in favor of the other. And management has the task of representing the library to the political world. Whereas public services staff may interact largely with library users, management has to talk to decision-makers who may be more skeptical or less informed about the library's actions and value.

Boundary-Spanning Stakeholders

As noted above, internal versus external is a continuum, not a dichotomy. Boundary spanners are those individuals at the boundary between the organization and its environment. Above, we described public services staff, as boundary-spanners because they often act as the interface between the library and the user. But as employees, they are clearly more internal to the organization than the following groups.

Trustees and board members. Many, though not all, public libraries have boards whose role is to represent the interests of the community, to the library, and the library to the community, that is, they act as boundary-spanners between the library and the community, and the library and local officials. As boundary-spanners, they take on some of the characteristics of people on each side of the boundary.

In the Public Library Effectiveness Study, trustees were most concerned with Internal Processes, Community Fit, and Traditional Counts. They are responsible for the library's relations with its public and for monitoring internal operations—usually either hiring and firing the director, or advising the government official who does so. And as quasi-members of the organization, they are probably more familiar with the traditional counts than others would be. In many instances the library will have used the Traditional Counts to communicate with its trustees.

Friends. Many libraries have formal friends of the library groups. These are volunteers who are active in supporting the library politically and financially (e.g., fund-raising). They are generally library users, but not average users: rather, they are "true-believer users." They are, by definition, strongly identified with the library as it is now.

Members of friends groups were most concerned with Community Fit, Services, and Access to Materials—fairly similar to users, of whom they are a dedicated subset.

Conclusion

The way to use the preference matrix (see figure 21, "Stakeholders' Preferences for Indicators") for talking with library stakeholders is to see it as a *general* guide to making choices about what to present. You will want to invent, create, adjust, rearrange, reject, refute. Hold in mind that your particular situation may not match— may actually contradict—the national data on which AMPLE and the matrix were built. The wrong way to use the matrix is to consider it an accurate picture of your particular situation. AMPLE and the matrix are checklists, not edicts. Your stakeholders may vary in their preferences from the national picture. And, of course, you will identify stakeholders differently from or more specifically than the seven in the matrix.

This chapter has considered how the library can communicate with its many constituent groups. We have talked in general about the information that constituent groups need and in what form, and specifically about who are the public library's constituents and what do we know about their interests and preferences.

The critical point is that the library has to address its audience's interests in terms that they understand. These interests may—probably will—vary across constituent groups. AMPLE is a help in designing an assessment program and using it to communicate with the library's environment, but in each situation local needs and preferences will determine what information is used and how. We can offer suggestions and

guidelines. But just as the movement in public libraries during the last 20 years or so has been toward local planning and measurement, so are assessment and communication ultimately functions of the local environment.

References

Chase, Gordon, and Elizabeth C. Reveal. 1983. *How to Manage in the Public Sector.* Reading, Mass.: Addison-Wesley.

Colorado State Library and Adult Education Office. 1991. "Salaries of Many Public Library Directors in Western States Fail to Keep Pace with Inflation." *Fast Facts* ED3/110.10/no. 49 (August 14).

Free Library of Philadelphia Foundation. 1991. "Five-Year Plan Brochure." Philadelphia: Free Library of Philadelphia.

Hasenfeld, Yehskel. 1983. *Human Service Organizations.* Englewood Cliffs, N.J.: Prentice-Hall.

Heymann, Philip B. 1987. *Politics of Public Management.* New Haven, Conn.: Yale University Press.

MacRae, Duncan, Jr. 1985. *Policy Indicators: Links between Social Science and Public Debate.* Chapel Hill: University of North Carolina Press.

McAuley, J. V. 1991. "Clubs." *Egg* (December/ January): 57–64.

Mills, Peter K. 1986. *Managing Service Industries: Organizational Practices in a Postindustrial Economy.* Cambridge, Mass.: Ballinger.

Mintzberg, Henry. 1989. *Mintzberg on Management: Inside Our Strange World of Organizations.* New York: Free Press.

"Peer Institution Data for Auraria Library, 1990." 1991. Denver: Colorado State Library and Adult Education Office (unpublished manuscript).

Pfeffer, Jeffrey, and Gerald R. Salancik. 1978. *The External Control of Organizations.* New York: Harper and Row.

Tufte, Edward R. 1990. *Envisioning Information.* New York: Graphics Press.

Van House, Nancy A., and Thomas Childers 1991. "Prospects for Public Library Evaluation." *Public Libraries* 30 (September/October): 274–78.

Wilson, James Q. 1989. *Bureaucracy: What Government Agencies Do and Why They Do It.* New York: Basic.

Wurman, Richard Saul. 1989. *Information Anxiety: What to Do When Information Doesn't Tell You What You Need to Know.* New York: Bantam.

And, in Sum . . .

8

Wherein the major points made in the preceding are recapped and the implications for the library future are drawn.

The mission of this book has been to (1) define effectiveness for the public library, and (2) provide guidelines for assessing the library's effectiveness and communicating it to the library's stakeholders.

Several themes have surfaced. First is that the task of the library manager vis-à-vis effectiveness is threefold: to manage an effective organization; to assess the library's effectiveness, without which the manager cannot judge success at the first task; and, finally, to communicate the library's effectiveness to the larger environment. This book emphasizes the last two, *assessing* and *communicating* the library's effectiveness. As a tax-supported organization, the library relies for its support on people who are not necessarily consumers of its services. The holders of the purse strings have to be informed of what good the library is accomplishing with the resources that they give it.

A second theme is that the decision-making process surrounding the library is political, with many players in various and shifting roles. The library has to identify them, address their interests, and communicate to them on their terms.

The third theme is that effectiveness is a big territory with many possible ways to map it, all of which are valid, all of which may be applied to the library at some time or another.

Effectiveness Defined

Chapter 1 begins by asking a basic question: "What is organizational effectiveness?" and defines it broadly as "goodness," the degree to which success has been achieved, the quality of an organization's performance.

Effectiveness can be assessed at many levels—the individual, the unit, or the organization. The emphasis in this book has been on organizational-level assessment, although the same concepts and methods can be and are used for units within the organization. Current methods of personnel evaluation, in addition, follow a similar approach in defining criteria, collecting information, and comparing the evidence on employee performance with expectations.

Libraries' growing concern with effectiveness comes, in part, because they are caught in a squeeze of rising costs and expectations and increasing competition for public funds. The basic issue is scarcity: there has never been and never will be enough funding for what the library can and should do. Libraries are caught in a continuing spiral of trying to do more with less. Society feels an increasingly urgent concern about getting the maximum benefit from its overstretched tax dollars. Taxpayers and government officials want to know the yield on their public investment. They want to know that the funds have been used wisely and that the programs they support are of value. As social problems intensify, people grow suspicious of established approaches. They doubt our ability to educate troubled youths, to halt the spread of drugs and crime, to fix our streets. They question not just the efficiency, but the efficacy, of public programs: Do the professionals really know what they are doing?

The management literature offers four main approaches to effectiveness. The *goal model* defines effectiveness in terms of the organization's achievement of specific ends. The *process model* is concerned with internal processes and organizational health. The *systems resource model* emphasizes the organization's need to secure resources from its environment. And the *multiple constituencies model* defines effectiveness as the degree to which the needs and expectations of the organization's constituent groups are met.

These models are not mutually exclusive, and all four surface in this book at various times. The library management tools developed by the Public Library Association—*Output Measures for Public Libraries* (Van House and others 1987) and *Planning and Role Setting for Public Libraries* (McClure and others 1987)—have taken a primarily goals-oriented approach, so that is the one probably the most familiar to most public librarians. But effectiveness has all these many faces. No single definition or approach is the most valid; in listening to constituents, the library manager may hear them all.

Evaluation

Chapter 2 looks at the process of evaluation and its relationship to effectiveness. Evaluation is judgment, the comparison of organizational performance against expectations and standards. Evidence of the organization's performance—objective and subjective, data, anecdotes, and impressions—provides the raw material for evaluation, but is not in itself evaluative.

Chapter 2 also defined some basic concepts. A *dimension* of effectiveness is a broad, underlying aspect of an organization's performance that is monitored in assessing effectiveness. A dimension is made up, in turn, of more specific items, or *indicators*. A dimension is more abstract and conceptual (for example, community fit), an indicator more concrete (for example, community awareness of library service offerings). An indicator is then operationalized by a *measure* (for example, proportion of respondents to a survey who are aware that the library lends videotapes). Each dimension may have multiple indicators, and each indicator may be operationalized in a variety of measures.

Ultimately, we want to know what causes effectiveness—what organizational actions work, what environmental characteristics have to be taken into account, and so forth. But to investigate this question, we have to determine how we will know success when we see it. That is, we first need to define and operationalize the dimensions, indicators, and measures of effectiveness.

The general systems model links inputs to processes to outputs to outcomes. In viewing an organization, we would like to have data about all of them, but inputs and processes are generally much easier to observe than outputs and outcomes. Orr (1973) shows how we assume that more library inputs will result in more and better outputs (services) and, ultimately, better outcomes (beneficial effects)—for example, we assume that more programs for youth-at-risk in branches in neighborhoods with a large number of such young people will bring them into the library and help them stay in school.

In assessing the library, observers apply their own criteria and operate from their own models of cause and effect concerning library services and community outcomes. For example, the city council member whose greatest concern is helping youth-at-risk may be most interested in the number of youth using the library because she assumes that library use will help them stay in school and, in turn, get gainful employment.

Existing measures of library services tend to be heavy on inputs and processes because they are readily observable and quantifiable. Although they are really only the means to achieve the ends (that is, outputs and outcomes), we use them as proxies for the ends.

Measurement data are not the only, or necessarily the best, way to evaluate organizational performance. Anecdotes are persuasive and memorable. Stories can illustrate and bring immediacy to data.

Management Tools

Chapter 3 shows how several major management tools fit into effectiveness, its assessment, and its presentation. Planning, measurement, budgeting, and personnel appraisal can all be understood as efforts toward assessing effectiveness and controlling action. Since the 1970s, the public library profession has been developing approaches to planning and measurement that can be used to assess effectiveness, as it is locally defined. Centrally defined standards of performance gave way to efforts to identify a single definition or measure of goodness which, in turn, gave way to a localization of planning and evaluation. Through such tools as *Planning and Role Setting for Public Libraries* (McClure and others 1987) and *Output Measures for Public Libraries* (Van House and others 1987), the Public Library Association has helped local libraries define effectiveness and assess it.

These works have their limits. They assume a rational, monolithic approach to decision-making that doesn't accurately reflect the library's complex political reality. However, they have improved the quality of data for decision-making in public libraries. They have provided not only a process, but an orientation toward defining the ends to be achieved and using quantitative data to assess progress.

Budgeting is also an essential way of representing an organization's effectiveness. Increasingly complex budgeting systems have emerged from the desire for greater accountability in the public sector. Government officials and the public want to know what they are getting for their money, in order to make difficult decisions about resource allocation. Budgeting systems are intended to show the relationship among inputs, processes, outputs, and outcomes.

Individual performance appraisal in many ways parallels organization-level performance appraisal. The library fulfills its mission, ultimately, through the people who work in it. Just as the organization is held accountable for what it accomplishes, so are the individuals within it. Newer appraisal methods link individual performance to organizational performance.

The Public Library Itself

Chapter 4 looks at several key characteristics of the public library. The first is that it is publicly funded. As a result, its income is determined by the political process, rather than coming from the sale of its services, so its income is separated from its outputs. The people making decisions about the library are not necessarily the ones who benefit. The library's budget is just one of a series of decisions negotiated by local government officials, interest groups, and other political players. As a result, the library may sometimes be seen as a bit player in a much larger drama. And the public library is not a major political player. It generally does not have either powerful foes or champions.

It may be difficult for the political decision-makers to decide how much to spend on the library. There is no common metric by which to assess the value of its outputs compared to its costs. The library's value to the larger community may not be as self-evident as that of the public services with which it competes—the police department, the fire department, social welfare agencies, and so forth.

The second characteristic is that the library is a service organization. Services—as opposed to goods—are often intangible and transitory, and difficult to observe and assess. Service is often a result of a partnership between the client and the service provider, each of whom plays a role in determining the outcome. The relationship between staff actions and client outcomes is often uncertain, that is, the best course of action is not always clear. And we can't really measure what interests us most: outcomes. The final effects of library use often occur later, outside of the library. Did the information obtained from the library help the client?

A third characteristic is that much library use is self-service. The library provides facilities, materials, and staff. Clients decide on their own how to use them, how far to go, and whether and when to ask for help. When we assess library effectiveness, then, we are assessing the interaction of the library and the client. Although the library has a responsibility to facilitate user success, the user plays a critical role in determining the purposes for which the library will be used and the result of his or her use of the library.

A Model of Public Library Effectiveness

Chapter 5 presents the major results of the Public Library Effectiveness Study. It was an empirical study of how public library constituents view public library effectiveness. We were not concerned with how effective they judged their libraries to be, but rather with the criteria they used in making those effectiveness judgments. Seven major public library constituent groups were asked to rate the importance of 61 indicators of public library effectiveness in evaluating the library. From their responses, rankings of the indicators for each of the seven groups were developed, and the indicators were grouped into eight broader dimensions of public library effectiveness. The dimensions can be used to define the larger issues to be addressed in assessing public library effectiveness and to choose among the indicators and their measures.

Chapter 6 presents "A Model of Public Library Effectiveness" (AMPLE), derived from the findings of the Public Library Effectiveness Study. AMPLE is a listing and classification of indicators and measures, grouped by dimensions, that may be used to review the comprehensiveness of a library's program of assessment, to develop a program of assessment, and to develop a strategy for communicating with key stakeholders. AMPLE is presented in both a longer and a shorter version, for the more and the less ambitious readers. It is not intended to be a ready-made assessment program, because each library must consider its own priorities and those of its community; but it does assist the library in improving its own assessment, decision-making, and communication with stakeholders.

AMPLE differs from *Output Measures for Public Libraries* (Van House and others 1987) in that the latter presented a very limited number of widely applicable measures of *output*. OMPL was designed to provide detailed hand-holding for a set of measures considered to be almost universally applicable to public libraries. AMPLE is designed to help in creating a more comprehensive and customized system of assessment. AMPLE may well be, for most libraries, the next step after *OMPL*.

Using AMPLE with Stakeholders

AMPLE = Assess and communicate library effectiveness.

To communicate with the many groups who assess the library and control its resources, or who influence those who do, the library has to identify the stakeholders, determine which indicators and measures will be most useful in communicating with them, and design a communication strategy.

Chapter 7 discusses some general principles for communicating with stakeholders, identifies the public library's major stakeholder groups, and identifies, from the Public Library Effectiveness Study and other sources, those groups' likely interests in the public library.

The final choice of indicators is largely political. Generally, political decision-makers are most concerned about how the service or program affects their constituents' interests—the larger problems of society and their particular concerns—and who is to benefit, what alliances are to be built, and the health of the political process. Library management has to decide who the audience is and what it wants to know.

The information that the library uses to describe itself to the larger world tells people what and who the library thinks is important, what the library has done and has tried to do, and for whom. Therefore, the library must build its asessment program to meet the agendas of its stakeholders. This does not mean that the library doesn't have its own agenda. Indeed, the library is given unusual latitude in setting its own agenda because most members of the larger community have a fairly simplistic idea of what the library should do and relatively low expectations for its performance.

The library must also argue for its own legitimacy—that it is using public funds wisely, for worthwhile programs and efficient operations. Because so many of its observers have a rather limited concept of the library, library management can, to a large degree, control their expectations, set their criteria, and influence their evaluation by the way that it presents itself.

In communicating about the library with external stakeholders, in particular, you should remember that people integrate new information with what they already know. Information needs to be presented in language they understand, and put into a familiar context. For example, comparisons give data a context, as when one neighborhood is compared with another. Local government, for instance, is especially concerned with spatial data and neighborhood comparisons.

Graphics can be particularly powerful for conveying information quickly and succinctly when used well. Stories and anecdotes are also powerful. They are easily remembered and can enliven data in ways that connect with the hearers' own experiences (for example, losing the equivalent cost of three fire trucks in disappearing library materials).

From the Public Library Effectiveness Study survey and interviews, and other discussion about public sector decision-making, we can infer some things about what is most likely to capture the interest of various stakeholder groups. However, each library has to consider its own community and the interests and needs of its particular stakeholders.

One of the more surprising findings is that the set of indicators that libraries have most commonly used (the Traditional Counts dimension) is of interest primarily to internal (librarian and trustee) stakeholders, but is not particularly interesting to anyone else. Externals are much more interested in the library's relationships with its community and its overall program of services. Externals also have a strong interest in the library's management. This is probably a manifestation of an overarching concern about the efficiency of government operations. What this means is that the library has to be careful to speak to its constituents about what it is doing and how, the results of its actions, and its internal operations.

Final Thoughts

The purpose of this book has been to help librarians become more effective managers and politicians. The two are indivisible. Running an efficient and effective operation is a necessary, but not a sufficient, condition for organizational health. The resources needed to keep the library going—funding, staff energy, users, and community support—depend not only on the library being good, but on others knowing that it is good.

The point is that a varied audience, with disparate understandings of the library, plays a critical role in determining the library's survival. The public library manager has to determine who audience members are and how to talk to them about the library. They have to see how the library is important to their interests. It is not enough today, if it ever was, to present the library in terms of how well it does what libraries are supposed to do. We cannot assume that people understand and value the public library simply on its own terms. The traditional community support for the public library as a good thing to have, regardless of who used it or for what, is giving way to the reality of overwhelming social problems, rising costs, overstressed tax revenues, and government deficits. In this kind of a climate, the public librarian has to be an astute manager and politician.

The managers of the public library have to be at least as critical and skeptical of the library as their audiences are. They have to be the first, not the last, to identify outmoded services and operations and to know when it is time to redirect the library. Those who believe that the public library is a valuable institution and have dedicated their careers to it have to be the most creative in adapting the library to the society that it serves and on which it depends, and in explaining the library to those who matter.

References

McClure, Charles R., Amy Owen, Douglas L. Zweizig, Mary Jo Lynch, and Nancy A. Van House. 1987. *Planning and Role Setting for Public Libraries.* Chicago: American Library Association.

Orr, Richard H. 1973. "Measuring the Goodness of Library Services: A General Framework for Considering Quantitative Measures." *Journal of Documentation* 29, no. 3: 315–32.

Van House, Nancy A., Mary Jo Lynch, Charles R. McClure, Douglas L. Zweizig, and Eleanor Jo Rodger. 1987. *Output Measures for Public Libraries,* 2nd ed. Chicago: American Library Association.

Appendices

A. The AMPLE Worksheet

The complete AMPLE model is repeated in this section for your use as a planning tool if desired. To use the "short" AMPLE, use only the measures highlighted with a gray background.

In this format, columns indicating other sources of measures have been eliminated. The columns indicating ease of use have been retained. Two narrow blank columns have been added at right for any use you may designate. Finally, the right-most "Comments" column is provided for your additional notes in planning an assessment project or any additional notations.

	E+	E	D	D+				Comments
Dimension 1: Traditional Counts								
1.1 USES AND USERS								
Total uses of all services per annum		x						
Current registration per capita	x							
Total users per annum per capita			x					
1.2 VISITS TO LIBRARY								
Annual visits (turnstile count)	x	x						
Frequency of visits per visitor			x					
Time spent in building			x					
Average number of services used during visits			x					
1.3 CIRCULATION								
Number of materials circulated per annum	x							
. . . and per capita	x							
Number of materials circulated per person per visit		x						
Types of materials borrowed per annum	x							
Total materials used		x						

	E+	E	D	D+				Comments
1.4 TOTAL EXPENDITURES								
Total annual expenditure	x							
Annual capital expenditure	x							
Annual operating expenditure	x							
Annual income by source	x							
1.5 REFERENCE VOLUME								
Number of reference transactions per annum	x							
Patterns of reference usage		x	x					
1.6 VARIETY OF USERS								
Users (grouped by demographic characteristics)	x							
as a percentage of total users	x							
as a percent of the population in each group	x							
1.7 MATERIALS TURNOVER								
Turnover rate	x							
Turnover rate by type of material	x							
1.8 MATERIALS EXPENDITURE								
Materials expenditure per annum	x							
. . . and + total operating expenditures	x							
Materials expenditure by category + total operating expenditures	x							
1.9 PROGRAM ATTENDANCE								
Program attendance per annum (audience size)	x							
Attendance at out-of-library programs	x							

	E+	E	D	D+				Comments

1.10 IN-LIBRARY USE

	E+	E	D	D+			Comments
In-Library use of materials	x						
. . . and as a % of circulation	x						

1.11 MATERIALS OWNED   Includes book, serial, audio, visual, microform, and computer formats

	E+	E	D	D+			Comments
Items held	x						
Items by type, as a % of total items	x	x					

1.12 STAFF SIZE

	E+	E	D	D+			Comments
Staff size	x						
Professional staff size per capita	x						
Number of staff + circulation	x						
Number of public service staff + users per annum		x					
Public service staff per hour open	x						

1.13 REFERENCE FILL RATE

	E+	E	D	D+			Comments
Reference fill rate		x					
Correct answers to reference questions			x				
Scope and depth of reference resources	x						

1.14 STAFF EXPENDITURES

	E+	E	D	D+			Comments
Expenditure for personnel	x						
. . . and as % of total expenditures	x						

1.15 EQUIPMENT USAGE

	E+	E	D	D+			Comments
Number of pieces of equipment available, by type		x					
Number of equipment uses		x					
. . . and per annum		x					
Percentage of time equipment is in use		x					

	E+	E	D	D+				Comments
1.16 Use of Library Compared to Other Services/Events Library uses per annum compared to other product or service use		x						

Dimension 2: Internal Processes

	E+	E	D	D+				Comments
2.1 Managerial Competence Managerial competence	x			!				
2.2 Staff Morale Staff morale	x		x					
2.3 Staff Quality Overall staff quality	x			!				
Total professionals + total staff	x							
2.4 Staff Helpfulness Helpful, courteous staff, concerned about client	x			x				
Level of staff assistance to users	x			x				
2.5 Support of Intellectual Freedom Library endorsement of intellectual freedom statements	x							
Use of materials regardless of content, format, or treatment, by any user	x							

	E+	E	D	D+			Comments
2.6 CONTRIBUTION OF LAYOUT, CATALOG, AND SIGNAGE TO SELF-USE (Indicator #63)							
"Transparency" of building layout		x	x				
Utility of catalog		x		x			
Utility of internal signage		x		x			
2.7 GOAL ACHIEVEMENT							
Extent to which formal library objectives are achieved	x						
2.8 EFFICIENCY OF LIBRARY OPERATIONS							
Operating expenditures per capita	x						
Operating expenditures + number of total client uses per annum		x					
Number of materials processed + dollars expended on materials processing		x					
Operating expenditures + library activity index or workload level			x				
2.9 WRITTEN POLICIES							
Existence of written policies	x						
2.10 SAFETY OF USERS							
Security of users of building, inside and outside	x						

Dimension 3: Community Fit

	E+	E	D	D+			Comments
3.1 COMMUNITY AWARENESS OF OFFERINGS							
Community awareness of library services			x				

	E+	E	D	D+				Comments
3.2 Users' Evaluation User evaluation of service received		x	x					
. . . immediately upon receiving the service		x	x					
. . . after using the information/ knowledge		x	x					
3.3 Contribution to Community Well-Being Contribution of library to community well-being		x		x				
Contribution of library to individual well-being				x				
. . . and to subgroups (e.g., business, students, etc.)				x				
Contribution to education of community				x				
Return on investment				!				
3.4 Services Suited to the Community Suitedness of services to community	x		x					
Extent to which target populations are reached		x	x					
3.5 Public Opinion Public opinion of library			x					
3.6 Flexibility of Library Management Adaptability of the organization and of management		x						
Adoption of innovation, both number and speed			x					

	E+	E	D	D+			Comments

3.7 STAFF SUITED TO THE COMMUNITY

Demographics of staff compared with demographics of population — E: x

Ability of staff to serve community — E: x

3.8 STAFF CONTACT WITH USERS

Number of contacts between users and service staff — E: x

Proportion of hours open when staff is available at service points — E: x

3.9 PUBLIC RELATIONS

Number of public relations events per annum — E: x

Qualified staff member(s) assigned to public relations — E+: x

Amount of staff time spent on public relations — E: x

3.10 RELATIONS WITH COMMUNITY AGENCIES

Number of formal groups served per annum — E: x

Number of non-service interactions with other agencies' service points — E: x

3.11 COMMUNITY ANALYSIS

Utilization of community studies in library decisions — E+: x, D+: x

---

Dimension 4: Access to Materials

4.1 COOPERATION WITH OTHER LIBRARIES

Cooperative activities with other libraries, including state library agency — E+: x

Membership in a formal library cooperative — E+: x

	E+	E	D	D+				Comments
4.2 SPEED OF SERVICE								
Turnaround hours for service requests			x					
Turnaround days for reserves, interlibrary and intrasystem borrowings		x						
User satisfaction with turn-around time			x					
4.3 INFORMATION ABOUT OTHER COLLECTIONS								
Subscriptions to state-wide, regional, or national holdings databases, manual or electronic		x						
4.4 INTERLIBRARY LOAN								
Number of interlibrary (i.e., intersystem) borrowings per annum	x							
Interlibrary borrowings fill rate		x						
4.5 MATERIALS AVAILABILITY								
Fill rates by types of search (subject, author, title, browsing, homework)		x						
Probability of materials ownership			x					
Availability of materials owned			x					
Overall user success rate			x					
4.6 EXTENT SERVICES ARE FREE								
Variety of services, materials, and facilities available free of charge	x							

	E+	E	D	D+			Comments

Dimension 5: Physical Facilities

	E+	E	D	D+			Comments
5.1 CONVENIENCE OF BUILDING LOCATION Convenience of site	x		x				
5.2 BUILDING EASY TO IDENTIFY Building clearly identifiable from the street	x						
5.3 PARKING Number of parking spaces	x		x				
Availability of parking spaces			x				
5.4 BUILDING SUITABILITY Square footage per capita	x						
Seating capacity per capita	x						
Suitability of furniture and equipment			x				
Intensity of use of facilities		x					
5.5 BUILDING APPEAL Appeal of library interior	x	x					
. . . and of library exterior	x	x					

Dimension 6: Boundary Spanning

	E+	E	D	D+			Comments
6.1 POLITICAL AND FISCAL VIABILITY OF THE LIBRARY (Indicator #62) Ratio of actual revenue to potential library revenue			x				
Size of budget compared to similar libraries		x					
Stability of funding		x					
Political success of the library	x						

	E+	E	D	D+				Comments
6.2 BOARD ACTIVENESS								
Activeness of library board	X							
Orientation of new board members	X							
Written bylaws for board, reviewed regularly	X							
6.3 VOLUNTARY CONTRIBUTIONS (Gifts, Money, Time)								
Dollar value of gifts of money, materials, equipment		X						
Hours of volunteer time per annum		X						
Dollars raised through effort of volunteers		X						
Activeness of Friends or other volunteers in the library's political arena	X							
6.4 LIBRARY PRODUCTS (Booklists, Guides, etc.)								
Number of library productions, publications, and recordings distributed per annum per capita	X							
6.5 ENERGY EFFICIENCY OF BUILDING								
Energy efficiency			X					
Participation in a recycling program	X							
6.6 CONTINUING EDUCATION FOR STAFF								
Number of hours of continuing education attended + staff member		X						
Number of continuing education events attended per staff member		X						
Percentage of staff participating in continuing education		X						

	E+	E	D	D+			Comments
6.7 PLANNING AND EVALUATION							
Long-range, written plan	x						
Long-term assessment of space needs	x						
Annual review and adjustment of plan	x						
Evaluation of library activities and programs	x						
6.8 PUBLIC INVOLVEMENT IN LIBRARY DECISIONS							
Defined mechanism for community input to design and development of services and facilities	x						
Complaints procedure for users		x					
Public access to board meetings and board documents		x					

Dimension 7: Service Offerings

	E+	E	D	D+			Comments
7.1 RANGE OF MATERIALS							
Variety of formats of materials		x					
Number of items in each format	x	x					
Breadth of subjects in library's collections		x					
Depth of holdings in library's collections			x				
7.2 RANGE OF SERVICES							
Number of services offered	x						
Extent to which library offers all of its services when open	x						
Innovative program of services	x						
7.3 CONVENIENCE OF HOURS							
Number of hours open per week	x						
Range of hours open	x						

(continued)

	E+	E	D	D+				Comments
7.3 (continued) Convenience to users of hours open			x					
Users, by hour			x					
7.4 MATERIAL QUALITY Collection quality			x					
7.5 NEWNESS OF MATERIALS Median publication date			x					
New volumes per annum	x							
. . . and per capita	x							
Titles added as a % of total titles, per annum	x							
Speed of acquisitions		x						

Dimension 8: Service to Special Groups

	E+	E	D	D+				Comments
8.1 HANDICAPPED ACCESS Handicapped accessibility		x	x					
8.2 SPECIAL GROUP SERVICES Services to populations with special needs		x	x					

B. Checklist of Library Services

Access to online databases
Adult programs
Assistance in borrowing materials from other libraries
Audio cassettes to circulate
Best-sellers, popular materials
Bookmobile service
Books by mail
Children's programs
Community bulletin boards
Equipment to use with films, records, tapes
Films to circulate
Help with homework
Help with reading skills
Help with selecting library materials (books, films, tapes, video tapes, etc.)
In-depth research materials
Magazines
Meeting rooms
Microcomputers for public use
Newspapers
Phonograph records to circulate
Photocopiers
Recreational reading
Reference/information

    Short answers to specific questions
    Assistance in locating material on a subject
    Assistance in developing search strategy
    Individual assistance in using the library or its materials, on demand
    Group or individual instruction in library or materials use
    Bibliographic verification of materials
    Preparation of subject bibliographies
    Referral to outside persons and organizations

Senior citizens' programs
Study/quiet space
Teenagers' programs
Video cassettes to circulate

Bibliography

Altman, Ellen, Ernest R. DeProspo, Philip M. Clark, and Ellen Connor Clark. 1976. *A Data Gathering and Instructional Manual for Performance Measures in Public Libraries*. Chicago: Celadon Press.

American Library Directory, 1991–1992. 1991. New York: R. R. Bowker.

Berelson, Bernard. 1949. *The Library's Public*. New York: Columbia University Press.

Bryant, Bonita. 1989. *Guide for Written Collection Policy Statements*. Chicago: American Library Association.

Bryson, John M. 1988. *Strategy Planning for Public and Nonprofit Organizations*. San Francisco: Jossey Bass.

Buckland, Michael K. 1988. *Library Services in Theory and Context*, 2nd ed. New York: Pergamon.

Cameron, Kim. 1981. "Domains of Organizational Effectiveness in Colleges and Universities." *Academy of Management Journal* 24: 25–47.

Chase, Gordon, and Elizabeth C. Reveal. 1983. *How to Manage in the Public Sector*. Reading, Mass.: Addison-Wesley.

Childers, Thomas, and Nancy A. Van House. 1989a. *The Public Library Effectiveness Study: Final Report*. Washington, D.C.: U.S. Department of Education, Office of Educational Research and Improvement.

Childers, Thomas, and Nancy A. Van House. 1989b. "Dimensions of Public Library Effectiveness." *Library and Information Science Research* 11 (July–September): 273–301.

Childers, Thomas, and Nancy A. Van House. 1989c. "The Grail of Goodness: The Effective Public Library." *Library Journal* 114 (October 1): 44–49.

Code of Federal Regulations 36, Chap. XI (July 1, 1990. Washington, D.C.: Office of the Federal Register, National Archives and Records Administration.

Colorado State Library and Adult Education Office, 1991. "Salaries of Many Public Library Directors in Western States Fail to Keep Pace with Inflation." *Fast Facts* ED3/110.10/no. 49 (August 14).

Damanpour, Fariborz, and Thomas Childers. 1985. "The Adoption of Innovations in Public Libraries." *Library and Information Science Research* 7 (July–September): 231–46.

D'Elia, George, and Eleanor Jo Rodger. 1991. *Free Library of Philadelphia Patron Survey: Final Report*. Philadelphia: Free Library of Philadelphia.

D'Elia, George, and Sandra Walsh. 1983. "User Satisfaction with Library Service—A Measure of Public Library Performance?" *Library Quarterly* 53 (April): 109–33.

DeProspo, Ernest R., Ellen Altman, and Kenneth E. Beasley. 1973. *Performance Measures for Public Libraries*. Chicago: American Library Association.

Free Library of Philadelphia Foundation. 1991. "Five-Year Plan Brochure." Philadelphia: Free Library of Philadelphia.

Hamburg, Morris, Richard C. Clelland, Michael R. W. Bommer, Leonard E. Ramist, and Ronald M. Whitfield. 1974. *Library Planning and Decision-Making Systems*. Cambridge, Mass.: MIT Press.

Hasenfeld, Yehskel. 1983. *Human Service Organizations*. Englewood Cliffs, N.J.: Prentice-Hall.

Hatry, Harry P., Louis H. Blair, Donald M. Fisk, John M. Greiner, John R. Hall, Jr., and Philip S. Schaenman. 1992. *How Effective Are Your Community Services? Procedures for Measuring Their Quality*, 2nd ed. Washington, D.C.: Urban Institute and the International City/County Management Association.

Heymann, Philip B. 1987. *Politics of Public Management*. New Haven, Conn.: Yale University Press.

Jobson, J. D., and Rodney Schneck. 1982. "Constituent Views of Organizational Effectiveness: Evidence from Police Organizations." *Academy of Management Journal* 25: 25–46.

Kaske, Neal, Annabel Stephens, and Philip Turner. 1986. "Alabama's Public Libraries as Seen by Patrons, Administrators, and Trustees." Tuscaloosa: University of Alabama (typescript).

King Research, Ltd. 1990. *Keys to Success: Performance Indicators for Public Libraries*. London: Office of Arts and Libraries.

Koenig, Michael E. D. 1980. *Budgeting Techniques for Libraries and Information Centers*. New York: Special Libraries Association.

Koenig, Michael E. D., and Vistor Alperin. 1985. "ZBB and PPBS: What's Left Now That the Trendiness

Has Gone?" *Drexel Library Quarterly* 21 (Summer): 19–38.

Lancaster, F. W. 1988. *If You Want to Evaluate Your Library . . . .* Champaign: University of Illinois.

MacRae, Duncan, Jr. 1985. *Policy Indicators: Links between Social Science and Public Debate.* Chapel Hill: University of North Carolina Press.

McAuley, J. V. "Clubs." *Egg* (December/January 1991): 57–64.

McClure, Charles R., Amy Owen, Douglas L. Zweizig, Mary Jo Lynch, and Nancy A. Van House. 1987. *Planning and Role Setting for Public Libraries.* Chicago: American Library Association.

Mills, Peter K. 1986. *Managing Service Industries: Organizational Practices in a Postindustrial Economy.* Cambridge, Mass.: Ballinger.

Minimum Standards for Public Library Systems, 1966. 1967. Chicago: American Library Association, Public Library Association, Standards Committee.

Mintzberg, Henry. 1989. *Mintzberg on Management: Inside Our Strange World of Organizations.* New York: Free Press.

Molz, Redmond Kathleen. 1990. *Library Planning and Policy Making: The Legacy of the Public and Private Sectors.* Metuchen, N.J.: Scarecrow Press.

Orr, Richard H. 1973. "Measuring the Goodness of Library Services: A General Framework for Considering Quantitative Measures." *Journal of Documentation* 29, no. 3: 315–32.

Osborne, David, and Ted Gaebler. 1992. *Reinventing Government: How the Entrepreneurial Spirit Is Transforming the Public Sector.* Reading, Mass.: Addison-Wesley.

Palmour, Vernon E., Marcia C. Bellassai, and Nancy V. DeWath. 1980. *A Planning Process for Public Libraries.* Chicago: American Library Association.

"Peer Institution Data for Auraria Library, 1990." 1991. Denver: Colorado State Library and Adult Education Office (unpublished manuscript).

Pfeffer, Jeffrey, and Gerald R. Salancik. 1978. *The External Control of Organizations.* New York: Harper and Row.

Public Library Data Service Statistical Report '90. Annual. Chicago: Public Library Association.

Robbins, Jane B., and Douglas L. Zweizig. 1992. *Keeping the Book$: Public Library Financial Practices.* Fort Atkinson, Wisc.: Highsmith Press.

Rubin, Howard. 1991. "Inch into Measurement." *Computerworld* (April 15): 79.

"Salaries of Many Public Library Directors in Western States Fail to Keep Pace with Inflation." 1991. *Fast Facts* ED3/110.10/no. 49 (August 14). Denver: Colorado State Library and Adult Education Office.

Schneier, Craig E., and Richard W. Beatty. 1979. "Combining BARS and MBO: Using an Appraisal System to Diagnose Performance Problems." *The Personnel Administrator* 24 (September): 51–60.

Scott, W. Richard. 1987. *Organizations: Rational, Natural, and Open Systems.* Englewood Cliffs, N.J.: Prentice-Hall.

Task Force on Federal-State Cooperative System for Public Library Data. 1989. *An Action Plan for a Federal-State Cooperative System for Public Library Data.* Washington, D.C.: U.S. National Commission on Libraries and Information Science; National Center for Education Statistics.

Tufte, Edward R. 1990. *Envisioning Information.* New York: Graphics Press.

Van House, Nancy A., and Thomas Childers. 1990. "Dimensions of Public Library Effectiveness II: Library Performance." *Library and Information Science Research* 12 (April–June): 131–53.

Van House, Nancy A., and Thomas Childers. 1991. "Prospects for Public Library Evaluation." *Public Libraries* 30 (September/October): 274–78.

Van House, Nancy A., and Thomas Childers. 1993. *The Public Library Effectiveness Study: The Complete Report.* Chicago: American Library Association.

Van House, Nancy A., Beth T. Weil, and Charles R. McClure. 1990. *Measuring Academic Library Performance: A Practical Approach.* Chicago: American Library Association.

Van House, Nancy A., Mary Jo Lynch, Charles R. McClure, Douglas L. Zweizig, and Eleanor Jo Rodger. 1987. *Output Measures for Public Libraries,* 2nd ed. Chicago: American Library Association.

Walter, Virginia. 1992. *Output Measures for Public Library Service to Children.* Chicago: American Library Association.

Wildavsky, Aaron. 1968. "Budgeting as a Political Process." In *International Encyclopaedia of the Social Sciences,* vol. 2. Macmillan & The Free Press.

Willett, Holly G. 1992. "Designing an Evaluation Instrument: The Environment Rating Scale in Process." *Journal of Youth Services in Libraries* 49, no. 2 (Winter): 165–73.

Wilson, James Q. 1989. *Bureaucracy: What Government Agencies Do and Why They Do It.* New York: Basic.

Wurman, Richard Saul. 1989. *Information Anxiety: What to Do When Information Doesn't Tell You What You Need to Know.* New York: Bantam.

Zammuto, Raymond F. 1984. "A Comparison of Multiple Constituency Models of Organizational Effectiveness." *Academy of Management Review* 9: 606–16.

Zweizig, Douglas L., and Eleanor Jo Rodger. 1982. *Output Measures for Public Libraries.* Chicago: American Library Association.

Index

Comments?

Now *you* tell *us* a story . . . about how you've been successful in assessing and communicating your library's effectiveness to your stakeholder groups.

Data you've used?

_____

_____

Stories and anecdotes?

_____

_____

Presentation methods?

_____

_____

Etc. . . .

_____

_____

_____

. . . and how have they worked?

_____

_____

_____

We'd love to hear. And if you have something to illustrate—a report to users, budget presentation, annual report—please send it!

_____

_____

_____

If you have any suggestion that would help make this book more useful, we'd like to hear that, too.

_____

_____

_____

Send to: Thomas Childers, College of Information Studies, Drexel University, Philadelphia, PA 19104.